WHISPERS FROM THE OTHER SIDE

A Comprehensive Guide to EVPs

STEVE HIGGINS

First edition published April 2023

ISBN 979-8-379-22394-6 (paperback)

Cover design by Jan Helebrant

Independently published by Project Weird
www.projectweird.com

PROJECT WEIRD

Contents

Introduction

Electronic Voice Phenomenon (EVP) is a fascinating and mysterious topic that has intrigued paranormal investigators for decades. EVPs are essentially unexplained human-like voices that are captured on electronic devices, such as audio recorders or radios. The source of these voices is unknown and is the subject of intense debate among paranormal investigators.

This book aims to provide readers with the knowledge and skills to capture high-quality EVPs and effectively analyse them. The book is suitable for both beginners and experienced ghost hunters who want to improve their knowledge of EVP research.

The source of these voices is still not fully understood, but it is widely believed that they are produced by spirits of the dead communicating with us. However, other theories suggest that the source of EVPs may be subconscious psychic projection, sounds from another dimension or time, or even simple audio interference.

Regardless of the cause of EVPs, conducting EVP sessions has become a common practice among ghost hunters. This book explains the methods used to capture and analyse EVPs, including how to use common audio recording equipment and audio editing software, how to deal with audio interference and unwanted sounds in recordings, and how to communicate with ghosts and spirits during an EVP session.

The book aims to provide readers with the knowledge and skills to form their own conclusions about the validity of EVPs. Rather than trying to prove or disprove that EVPs are genuine contact with spirits, the book focuses on giving readers the best chance of capturing high-quality EVPs and providing guidance on how to effectively analyse them.

To stand the best chance of capturing, understanding, and validating an EVP, it is important to use best practises when conducting EVP sessions, including being respectful and polite when communicating with spirits, using proper equipment, and taking precautions to ensure safety. You will also learn about the importance of maintaining objectivity when analysing EVP recordings and how to avoid confirmation bias.

I hope this book will serve as a comprehensive guide to EVP research, providing you with the knowledge and skills to capture and analyse high-quality EVP recordings. Whether you are a beginner or an experienced ghost hunter, this book is an essential resource for anyone interested in the mysterious and intriguing world of EVPs.

Defining Electronic Voice Phenomenon

The quality of EVPs varies from sounds like groans, whispers, and growls to clear, human-like voices in the form of an intelligible sentence or phrase. Sometimes amplification, noise filtering, or enhancement is used in order to hear the voices.

At their best, an EVP can be a recognisable voice. You'll be able to clearly identify words, and the tone of the voice will indicate whether the voice is likely to be that of a man, woman, or child. If clear enough, the pace, intention, or vocabulary may even allow you to identify the voice as a specific person. You may also be able to determine the state of mind of the speaker through the tone of their voice; the speech might sound angry, sad, or happy, for example.

Unfortunately, you're not likely to encounter this best-case scenario on every investigation. It's more likely the voices you capture will be gruff or made up of breathy groans, grunts, or even growling. The EVP is most likely to be one word, perhaps two or three, but whole sentences are rare and dialogues are almost unheard of.

Ideally, you are listening for intelligent or direct responses. These are words and phrases that directly respond to your questions, the current conversation in the room, or a statement that is timely or in context with what's going on in the environment.

The source of these voices is still not fully understood by paranormal investigators, and it is written off as pseudoscience by skeptics. Of course, many parapsychologists and paranormal investigators believe that EVPs are produced by the spirits of the dead communicating with us. It's said that these spirit voices can be unintentionally recorded or intentionally recorded on demand. There are also several other commonly shared theories relating to the source of EVPs, including subconscious psychic projection and sounds from another dimension or time.

Electronic Voice Phenomenon is a form of Instrumental Transcommunication (ITC). ITC is an umbrella term that refers to a wider field of spirit communication using any kind of electrical instrument that isn't just limited to voices.

The term "Instrumental Transcommunication" was coined in the 1970s by Prof. Ernst Senkowski, a scientist with a background in experimental physics who went on to conduct experiments to try to find out the source of unexplained voices on audio tapes.

The term "ITC" isn't limited to audio devices; it encompasses any communication between the living and spirits or any other supernatural entity through any electronic device. This can be anything from tape recorders through to computers, and in more recent years ghost hunting gadgets and smartphone apps.

ITC also covers visual forms of communication, normally conducted with the use of a television and video camera feedback loop, which creates the Droste effect, where a picture recursively appears within itself, or simply by observing patterns in static.

Today, ITC is more actively investigated by parapsychologists and spiritualists than ever before. The array of devices available to carry out experiments is endless. Modern paranormal investigators can get their hands on plenty of commercially available gadgets.

The first of these modern devices was the Frank's Box, named after its creator, Frank Sumption, which he developed in 2002. There are many similar devices available on the market today; they're now generally referred to as "ghost boxes" or "spirit boxes." The most common being the P-SB7 and P-SB11 spirit boxes.

Most spirit boxes work by scanning through the AM, MW, and FM radio spectrum. As it does, fleeting bursts of white noise and static can be heard. Spirit boxes usually have various settings that allow you to tweak which bands the device scans through and how much of each frequency step you hear; this usually ranges from a hundredth of a second up to a second. The belief is that spirits can use radio broadcasts as well as the white noise between the stations to communicate with the device's user.

Another popular modern form of ITC is electronic speech synthesis, like the Ovilus and Echovox. These types of devices can be quite expensive; however, there are cheaper versions available as apps for smartphones. They work as either random word generators or by generating random sounds, the phonics that make up words. It's said that spirits can affect the random nature of these devices to form intelligent responses to the user's questions.

Most devices of this type use atmospheric sensors to generate their random output. They monitor conditions such as temperature, pressure, humidity, and electromagnetic field strength. It uses these signals as a random number generator, and this number is used to reference a database of words or sounds. The atmospheric sensors give the spirits a way to influence the random nature of the output.

An EMF metre can also be used as a form of ITC, but only when used for communication as opposed to taking baseline electromagnetic field measurements or looking for EM spikes.

An EMF meter, or electromagnetic field meter, is one of the most popular pieces of ghost hunting equipment. They are simple to use, often consisting of nothing more than an on/off switch. They detect and alert you to fluctuations and spikes in EM flux, and the device gives instant feedback via a digital display or LED indicator.

In order to use an EMF metre to communicate with spirits, the user should encourage the spirits to come forward and try to trigger the lights on the EMF metre to show that they are present or to indicate an answer to a question.

These are just a few of the most commonly used electronic devices in the ITC field, but the list doesn't end here. Over the years, there have been reports of just about every type of electrical device being used to communicate with spirits, from telephones and fax machines through to battery-powered children's toys and flashlights.

Direct Voice Phenomenon

Electronic Voice Phenomenon shouldn't be confused with Direct Voice Phenomenon (DVP). DVP is sometimes also referred to as an AVP or Audible Voice Phenomena, but the terms are interchangeable.

DVPs are similar to EVPs in that they are disembodied voices that are heard during paranormal investigations, séances, or at a haunted location. The difference is that they are audible at the time and are spoken directly to the investigator or witness. No audio or electrical equipment is needed to hear a DVP; they are heard in real time with nothing more than the human ear.

Direct voice phenomena are much more rare than EVPs, almost as rare as full-bodied apparitions, but it's not uncommon for people to report hearing laughter, cries, or even menacing voices shouting "get out" while at an allegedly haunted property.

Although DVP relates to audible voices, the phenomenon shouldn't be confused with voices produced in cases like the famous Enfield Poltergeist haunting, when a gruff male voice seemed to be coming from Janet Hodgson. This is not a DVP, as in this case Janet was the instrument of communication, meaning it was not direct. That is why the phenomenon is called "direct voice" or "independent voice" - no equipment is involved, and the voice isn't spoken through a third party.

Although rare, DVPs are a concept that most investigators are familiar with and disembodied voices is something they are actively listening for during ghost hunts, but traditionally direct voice phenomenon was more closely associated with a unique branch of mediumship. In séances, it wasn't uncommon for a direct-voice medium to facilitate voice communication.

It was believed that the medium was able to encourage and give the spirit the energy to come forward and communicate, but sitters claimed that the voice didn't come from the medium themselves. Instead, it was heard coming from mid-air in front of the medium or elsewhere in the room, and the words were spoken in the spirit's own voice.

There are plenty of examples of spirits who are able to manifest audible voices. One of the best known cases is the tale of the ghost of Sarah Siddon, who is said to haunt the Bristol Old Vic theatre in England. The building is one of the oldest continually operating theatres in the world, built between 1764 and 1766.

Sarah's boyfriend hanged himself at this theatre, and her ghost is thought to continue to mourn the loss. Staff working at the theatre have reported hearing a female voice telling them to "get out," a classic example of a DVP.

The key to hearing a DVP during an investigation is to be patient and quiet and to offer lots of encouragement to the spirits. Call out and ask any spirits present at an allegedly haunted location to use their voice to talk to you. Ask them to use your energy to communicate and remember to encourage them and don't make demands of them. After calling out, stay still and quiet and give the spirits time to answer.

Of course, if you have recording equipment with you during an investigation and a DVP is heard, then there's a good chance that you could capture the audio in your recording. Recording a DVP doesn't make it an EVP, as by its definition, an EVP is a voice heard through electronic means only.

Residual vs. Intelligent Interactions

There's no agreed-upon mechanism that explains how voices are captured as EVPs; in fact, even the origins of these voices are disputed. One thing that most paranormal investigators agree upon is that most hauntings fall into one of two categories: residual hauntings or intelligent hauntings; these classifications may also be relevant to EVPs.

Residual Hauntings

Residual hauntings are a type of haunting where the witness is seeing, sensing, or experiencing the residual psychic or emotional energy of a person or an event that took place at that location in the past. For this reason, residual hauntings are sometimes called "place memories."

Residual hauntings are said to be an imprint of energy that has been left behind by someone who suffered a tragic, premature death, usually a murder, suicide, or execution. The belief is that the energy used by the body and the brain in resisting death can be so immense that those events can be replayed either on the anniversary of the event, when atmospheric conditions are similar, or when someone is susceptible to or in tune with that energy.

As residual hauntings represent nothing more than a reflection of the past, you can't communicate with them. The visions seen are not aware of their surroundings. They cannot interact with you and are not aware of your presence. They are benign and non-threatening.

A residual haunting can be a vision or even a sense of foreboding in a particular room or location where something traumatic has occurred, but it can also be audible. Residual hauntings can contain elements of sound, such as disembodied voices, but they can also be audio-only. There are many examples of audible residual hauntings, from phantom footsteps to the sounds of music playing in the courtyard of a castle or horses galloping across a battlefield.

It's not known whether these events replay for everyone or just those who are open to these types of energies or who have psychic abilities. This raises the question of whether an EVP could be an imprint or a recording of residual energy. If an EVP is residual, then there will be no intelligent spirit that is responsible for it, so the voices in the recording will be unable to understand you or answer back. This could be an indication that you are dealing with a residual haunting. This may also be the case if you capture footsteps, cries, laughter, or just about any other unexplained noise.

Intelligent Hauntings

Most, if not all, genuine EVPs are likely to be the result of intelligent hauntings, also known as interactive hauntings. In this type of haunting, a ghost or spirit may manifest or communicate in some way. Because there is believed to be an awareness or consciousness of sorts behind these ghosts, they are able to hear your questions and respond with relevant responses.

The goal of any EVP research is to capture intelligible responses that relay meaningful messages. For this to be the case, you would have to be dealing with an intelligent haunting.

Origins of the Voices

How an EVP is actually captured in a recording is still not understood by parapsychologists. Of course, what we do know is that ghosts and spirits don't have physical bodies; therefore, they have no vocal cords, so it could be argued that they can't produce a voice in the same way that living humans do.

However, this isn't strictly true. It's widely agreed upon by paranormal investigators that ghosts are sometimes able to move objects, slam doors, and break items. Therefore, they must at times be able to take a physical or partially physical form, or at the very least be able to manipulate the physical world around them. If this is the case then they may also have the ability to vibrate the air around them in order to make sounds, which are at a basic level vibrations in the air.

The idea that they can do this, either at will or under certain conditions, is backed up by the common belief that ghosts are also able to produce direct and audible voices; we hear the sound of their clothes rustling and even their footsteps.

In the early séances of the late 1800s, mediums believed that spirits were able to spontaneously form physical vocal cords to speak through using a substance called ectoplasm. This is one theory that could explain direct voice phenomena, but when it comes to EVPs, the voice isn't actually heard out loud, so it could be that the voice is imprinted in the recording using a kind of psychic energy or manufactured electrical interference.

No matter what method is used to make the recording, the leading theory about the origins of EVPs is that they are the voices of the dead - whether that be in the form of residual or intelligent spirits - this isn't the only theory. It's entirely possible that the voices heard in EVPs aren't voices of the dead but are, in fact, voices from another point in space, time, or a different dimension.

Many within the paranormal field believe that a portal or vortex can allow an entity to cross over into the physical world we live in from the plane of existence that ghosts inhabit - the spirit world. There's also a growing number of claims that they could be inter-dimensional gateways or even doorways to a different point in time, either the past or the future. This is based on claims that objects and artefacts have fallen through portals. Items like feathers, arrowheads, and ancient coins have been found in places where they have no business being.

The idea of other planes of existence isn't too far-fetched. There's growing support from leading scientists for the many-worlds interpretation, which suggests that there are one or more, perhaps an infinite number, of complete universes co-existing with us on a plane we are not aware of.

It's for this reason that some paranormal researchers believe that hauntings could be caused by beings from another dimension and that ghosts could be explained as beings living in one or more parallel dimensions. When conducting experiments with EVPs, it's just as likely that we are inadvertently communicating with living humans in a parallel universe as it is that we're communicating with the spirits of the dead.

It might not just be the barriers between realities that ghost hunters are breaking down but also those between space and time. Ghost hunts are usually conducted in haunted houses, castles, or other locations believed to be haunted. This means that over several years, many different groups of paranormal researchers focus their attention on the exact same location in an attempt to make contact with spirits. Some believe that it's possible that psychic energies from different time periods could be converging and could be what is causing spiritual contact and even the voices in EVP recordings.

If it isn't the spirit of the deceased that we're communicating with and it is, in fact, the focussed energy of ghost hunters from the past, then these people from the past have made contact with us here in their future. This means it could also be possible for today's ghost hunters to make contact with people in the future.

Communication between the dead and the living, or in this case, the two points in time, doesn't normally consist of a linear conversation; instead, it's a voice imprinted in an EVP recording, the movement of the planchette over a Ouija board, or tapping to indicate "yes" or "no." Perhaps this is because subconscious psychic energies are being drawn to each other. Those taking part in an investigation may not even realise what messages they're throwing out into the past or future.

Space and time is so intrinsically linked as the spacetime continuum, that if it's possible to communicate through time, then it should also be possible to communicate with different physical locations throughout the universe.

There's no real way to know where the voice in an EVP recording is coming from. Even if the voice identifies itself by giving you its name in the recording, this could mean you're communicating with the spirit of that person, but you could also be in communication with their living counterpart in an alternative reality.

Of course, as well as the many possible supernatural explanations, there are also plenty of natural explanations for EVPs. Skeptics maintain that EVPs are merely the result of poorly conducted recording sessions where unwanted noise is introduced through overamplification, noise reduction, or enhancement, which can cause recordings to take on qualities significantly different from those that were present in the original recording.

Other natural causes include interference from broadcast sources, including radio broadcasts, CB radio transmissions, transmissions from wireless baby monitors, sounds caused by the recording device being moved or handled, or the sounds of the inner workings of the recorder itself.

Subconscious Imprinting

A final theory on the origins of EVPs is that they're not coming from a spirit or another being at all; instead, they are audible imprints of the EVP practitioner's mental thoughts that are subconsciously recorded through psychokinesis, especially given that our thoughts are an electrochemical process in the brain.

Spirits are believed to be our souls or the energy that gives rise to our consciousness, which lives on outside the body. If we are willing to accept that this disincarnate energy is capable of affecting an audio recorder, then it could also be the case that the energy or soul within a living human can have the same effect.

The living are consciously aware of the intent of what they are about to say, as well as the words, before we form the sentence aloud. If a spirit's conscious energy works in the same way, then it's possible that it is this mental intent that causes an imprint in an audio recording. This means that a paranormal investigator who is focussing on the question they've just asked to the spirit could unwittingly mentally project the answer they hope for or expect onto the recording. It might be that the investigator is subconsciously willing the spirit to answer with a specific word or phrase.

Famous EVP researcher Konstantīns Raudive's work might have helped confirm that EVPs are the result of some form of psychic projection rather than an audible sound. He often used a germanium diode in a radio circuit to capture EVPs. Modern-day researchers now plug a similar diode into an audio recorder instead of a microphone. A germanium diode is a low-resistance electrical component and isn't capable of capturing audio in the same way that a microphone does. This means that any voices captured using this method were never audible.

If EVPs are a result of our own subconscious thoughts being imprinted in the recording, then it becomes harder to tell if the voices heard come from the depths of our psyche or from a spirit. In order to validate that a voice isn't the result of our own thoughts, the EVP would have to impart information that none of the investigators present are aware of and that can be validated later. This would help to prove that the voice hasn't come from the investigators themselves as they didn't have this information before-hand.

However, where information is known to an investigator or generic phrases are spoken in the EVP, it's impossible to rule out the fact that the EVP could be unwittingly caused by the investigator themselves. For this reason, when attempting to capture EVPs, you should aim to collect information that you are not aware of but that can be corroborated later. Information such as dates of birth, next of kin, or anything else that you could verify in records after the investigation.

If you want to explore this theory further, then you could try a psychic projection experiment. This involves using an audio recorder and intentionally focussing on one specific word that has been decided on in advance. You could either try this alone or with a group of people all concentrating on the same word. Leave the audio device recording for 30 to 60 seconds; this should be enough time for the imprint to occur without the need for you to review long audio recordings afterwards.

The person reviewing the audio shouldn't have been part of the original experiment and shouldn't be aware of the word in advance. It is their job to listen to the audio objectively and write down any words they hear. If the theory is correct, then the word they write down should match the one you decided upon before the experiment.

If the experiment is unsuccessful, continue to repeat it and retry it with a different word each time. EVPs aren't captured on every attempt and there's no scientific understanding of what allows them to be captured, so it may be that you have more luck in subsequent attempts.

Scalar Waves

Scalar waves are a proposed type of exotic energy that some paranormal investigators think could be linked to the transmission and capturing of EVPs.

Some believe that different frequencies of scalar waves are responsible for supernatural phenomena like telepathy and clairvoyance. So, it might be possible for mediums or those who are sensitive to be able to consciously or subconsciously pick up on scalar energy.

It's also been suggested that scalar waves could be the mechanism that imprints spirit voices in audio recordings, essentially powering EVPs.

The belief is that scalar waves can pass through ordinary matter, even right through the core of the Earth and out the other side. EVPs have been captured when the recording devices have been electromagnetically shielded in a Faraday pouch; this could be possible if the wave carrying an EVP could pass through an object such as a Faraday cage.

However, there's no agreed-upon scientific understanding of how this could work, but if scalar does represent an undiscovered branch of science, then this might mean that the principles and processes of scalar waves are still to be discovered and they could work in the way described.

Creating a device that can detect scalar waves is an interesting challenge, especially if the waves behave as they are said to. If scalar waves are able to pass through solid objects, including metals, then there is no way to detect them with an aerial made of metal. The waves shouldn't interact with any type of machine.

The current understanding in the scalar theory research community is that you'd have to detect a scalar wave's influence by measuring more conventional fields. In fact, most designs for scalar wave detectors take the approach of recording the unseen waves' effects on electromagnetic fields. If scalar can influence traditional electromagnetic waves, then it could influence electrical devices in such a way that voices could be transposed into recordings.

Scalar-wave research is still very new and generally not accepted by mainstream science. Scalar within the paranormal world is even more specialised, with just a handful of investigators experimenting with it.

The History of EVP Research

The spiritualist movement began in the 1840s, when holding a séance was the most common way to attempt to contact spirits, usually through a medium. This was about 100 years before audio recording technology was invented. As technology evolved, so did the methods used to attempt to contact spirits.

The first radio transmission had been made by the Italian inventor, Guglielmo Marconi, in 1895, and by the early 1900s, the possibility that radio-based equipment could be used to contact the dead was being explored.

Father Roberto Landell de Mour, a Brazilian Catholic priest and inventor who was an early pioneer in long-range radio broadcasting and voice transmission technologies, was the first to experiment with electronic spirit communication. In 1910, it's said that he laid the groundwork for future generations of ITC researchers when he demonstrated a device that produced EVPs through radio technology.

Landell's work is little more than a legend, and very little is known about his session in which he spoke to spirits. Even at the time, the inventor refused to talk about the inner workings of his device, as communicating with spirits through any other method than prayer is frowned upon in the Christian church.

However, it could also be seen as a little suspicious that the man, who some claim sent a voice transmission before even Marconi, had a box that was able to hear his questions when he spoke into it and answer back by producing a voice.

In the 1920s, the American inventor Thomas Edison fuelled the possibility that technology could be used to communicate with spirits. Edison was a prolific inventor who contributed to such technologies as the electric light, the phonograph, and the nickel-iron battery, but in 1920 he shared his belief that it may be possible to build a machine that could communicate with human personalities that live on after death.

In the article entitled 'Edison's Views on Life and Death' in the October 1920 edition of the magazine Scientific American, Edison said, "I have been thinking for some time of a machine or apparatus which could be operated by personalities which have passed on to another existence or sphere. Now follow me carefully; I don't claim that our personalities pass on to another existence or sphere."

He claimed that "it is possible to construct an apparatus so delicate that if there are personalities in another existence or sphere who wish to get in touch with us in this existence or sphere, that this apparatus will at least give them a better opportunity to express themselves."

Edison went on to state that he doubted other methods of spirit communication; he gave unreliable examples such as table tipping, rapping, Ouija boards, and mediumship. He said, "In truth, it is the crudeness of the present methods that makes me doubt the authenticity of purported communications with deceased persons. Why should personalities in another existence or sphere waste their time working a little triangular piece of wood over a board with certain lettering on it? Why should such personalities play pranks with a table? The whole business seems so childish to me that I frankly cannot give it my serious consideration. I believe that if we are to make any real progress in psychic investigation, we must do it with scientific apparatus and in a scientific manner, just as we do in medicine, electricity, chemistry, and other fields."

It seems that what Edison was proposing to do was give investigators a more scientific approach to spiritualism than the other more "crude methods" employed at the time. He said, "What I propose to do is to furnish psychic investigators with an apparatus that will give a scientific aspect to their work."

He described his vision of the apparatus as a valve-like device, probably similar to the type found in old vacuum tube radios. He said that it should be capable of massively amplifying even the slightest effort to effect it. This would make it much easier for a spirit to interact with it than sliding a planchette across a Ouija board or tipping a table.

In another article published on October 15th, 1920 in the Canadian news magazine Maclean's, Edison is quoted as saying, "I am engaged in the construction of one such apparatus now, and I hope to be able to finish it before very many months pass."

In the same publication, Edison is quoted as saying, "If our personality survives, then it is strictly logical and scientific to assume that it retains memory, intellect, and other faculties and knowledge that we acquire on this earth. Therefore, if personality exists, after what we call death, it is reasonable to conclude that those who leave this earth would like to communicate with those they have left here."

Thomas Edison died in 1931, having never completed the device or given any further information on the theory behind it or its operation.

Early EVP Recordings

As technology evolved, recording equipment became accessible, and with this innovation came attempts to capture spirit voices in recordings, the true origins of the modern-day EVP movement. It was an American psychic of Hungarian descent named Attila von Szalay who was at the forefront of this new approach.

At the time, Szalay was working as a photographer in California, where he specialised in spirit photography, the art of photographing ghosts or spirits. In 1941, to expand his work, he decided to attempt to capture the voices of spirits. He did this using one of the first commercially available home recording devices - the Packard Bell Phonocord.

The phonocord recorder cutter used an external microphone to record sounds to a 5-inch blank record spinning at 78 revolutions per minute. The device was also capable of playing back the recordings. From 1950 on, Szalay teamed up with psychologist Raymond Bayless, and together they continued experimenting, and in 1956 technology once again leaped forward and the researchers began using a reel-to-reel tape recorder.

They conduct their EVP experiments in much the same way as mediums did in early séances. A microphone was placed in an insulated spirit cabinet. The medium, in this case psychic Szalay, would sit in the cabinet in order to channel the spirits. The microphone was connected to the tape recorder, which was outside the cabinet.

The researchers found that they had captured many unexplained sounds in their recordings that were not heard during the experiment. Some of these sounds were recorded at times when there was no medium in the cabinet.

Reverend Charles Drayton Thomas, a British Methodist minister and spiritualist, also became one of the first to capture a spirit voice in a recording in the early 1940s. Thomas, a member of the Society for Psychical Research, was investigating the validity of a well-known medium of the time, Gladys Osborne Leonard. During one of their sessions together, Thomas found that he had captured on tape the disembodied voice of his own father.

The next leap forward in the field of EVP research came in 1959 when Friedrich Jürgenson, a painter and film producer from Sweden, captured what he thought sounded like voices on tape. The recording happened by accident while Jürgenson was attempting to record bird song in woodland.

Jürgenson concluded that the voice in the recording was clearly human, but was unable to ascertain how it had been recorded as the tape had been blank before, meaning it couldn't have been sound leaking through from a previous recording. The area of woodland he'd been in was very remote, which eliminated the possibility that someone made the sounds at the time of recording.

This led Jürgenson to investigate the phenomenon further. He was able to rule out the possibility of radio interference and eventually started to capture much longer phrases and sentences. He then found that the voices in his recordings started to address him by name, and he was able to identify one of the voices as that of his dead mother.

Later in his research, Jürgenson became the first to combine the technique of recording EVPs with the earlier method of radio contact in order to improve his results. Jürgenson went on to write two books on the subject of EVP, 'Rösterna Från Rymden' ('Voices from the Universe') published in 1964, and 'Radio och Mikrofonkontakt med de Döda' originally published in 1968, then translated into German as 'Sprechfunk mit Verstorbenen' ('Voice Transmissions With The Deceased') in 1981.

Agostino Gemelli also captured an unexplained voice on tape, and like Jürgenson, he captured the sounds inadvertently, and it was the sound of a deceased parent. Gemelli was an Italian Franciscan friar and former physician. He captured the voice in 1952 while working in Milan with Father Pellegrino Ernetti, an Italian priest and scientist.

The pair were attempting to record the sounds of Gregorian chants using a reel-to-reel tape recorder, but they were experiencing technical issues with the microphone. At one point during the recording session, Gemelli looked to the heavens and asked his dead father for help. When Gemelli and Ernetti later reviewed the tape, they heard a voice that Gemelli recognised as his dead father's, and that voice said, "Of course I shall help you. I'm always with you."

Konstantin Raudive

Inspired by the work of Jürgenson, the next big name in the field of paranormal research was Konstantin Raudive, a Latvian parapsychologist, writer, and student of the famous Swiss psychiatrist, Carl Jung.

Raudive got in contact with Jürgenson after reading his book and initially worked with him to capture EVPs in 1965. In one of these early experiments, Raudive heard multiple voices in a recording, with voices speaking in German, Latvian, and French. One of the voices said "va dormir, Margarete," which translates as "go to sleep, Margaret."

In his 1968 book on EVPs, 'Unhörbares Wird Hörbar' (translated into English as "what is inaudible becomes audible," but published in 1971 as 'Breakthrough: An Amazing Experiment in Electronic Communication with the Dead,') Raudive wrote, "These words made a deep impression on me, as Margarete Petrautzki had died recently, and her illness and death had greatly affected me."

Raudive also recorded the voice of a deceased parent. He heard his mother's voice using his childhood name, Kostulit: "Kostulit, this is your mother."

His early experiments drove Raudive to spend the next nine years of his life, until his death in 1974, exploring EVPs with the help of German parapsychologist Hans Bender. It's said that over his career he recorded more than 100,000 recordings. With a career that only spanned about a decade, this would mean that he'd have to have recorded around 30 EVPs per day.

Raudive used several methods of recording EVPs, each method was carried out in strict laboratory conditions, which included screening from external radio interference.

The most simple method employed by Raudive was to use a normal microphone connected to a tape recorder. He left this running in silence, with no one talking. At times he even used this method but without a microphone even connected to the recorder.

He also used a standard radio that was not tuned to any station so that it just produced white noise, which he would record and later analyse for voices. The voices obtained through this method are sometimes referred to as RVPs, or Radio Voice Phenomenon.

The third method was similar but used a modified radio. The method is known as "diode recording" and involves replacing the most important component in a simple crystal radio, the crystal detector, with a piece of germanium. This has become known as a germanium diode or Raudive diode.

The diode was too short to pick up radio transmissions and could not be tuned to a specific station; instead, it acted as a noise generator fed by a broad band of the radio spectrum. It was believed that this wide, untuned band of radio noise provided the raw energy required for the voice formation process.

In order to avoid his own subjectivity, Raudive invited more than 400 impartial volunteers to listen back to the voices he'd captured and to interpret them without bias - all of whom heard distinguishable voices.

Raudive's germanium diode was later put to use by businessman George Meek and his psychic research partner, William O'Neil. Together, they used a similar diode to develop the Spiricom device. At a 1982 press conference, the researchers demonstrated their radio-based device, which also used a tone generator spanning the frequency range of the human voice, and claimed that it made two-way communication with the dead possible.

They went on to record hundreds of hours of voices using this, but only when the device was used by O'Neil. Meek put this down to O'Neil's psychic abilities being an essential component of the system.

Marcello Bacci

One of the most fascinating cases of early EVP research was demonstrated by the Italian medium, Marcello Bacci. Starting in 1974, over a period of about 20 years, Bacci gave public performances of his spirit communication technology to audiences in Grosseto, Italy. Audience members were given the chance to hear the voices of their deceased loved ones.

Bacci started out by using an old military radio that was used on naval ships but eventually moved on to a larger vacuum tube radio set with three loudspeakers, which he said provided better sound and clearer voices. Both of these radios were unmodified.

During the demonstration, he would then tune the radio to a part of the radio spectrum that was devoid of radio broadcasts. In a 2000 interview, he explained, "There is not a particular frequency. I can go all the way from left to right and if the voices want, they come in." After ten to twenty minutes, the white noise from the speakers would die down and the voices of the spirits would clearly come through.

The voices are much clearer and more sustained than those captured by most other EVP researchers. Some of the voices Bacci's radio produced could deliver coherent dialogues that were several minutes long. They are easy to identify as male or female, and each voice sounded distinct and unique.

The most commonly retold explanation for Bacci's demonstration is that he had unique psychic abilities that the experiment relied upon. It's said to be for this reason that Bacci had to be in constant contact with the radio's dials during the demonstration. If he left the room at any point, the voices would stop. His radio also failed to produce results for anyone else who used it.

Many skeptics tried to debunk Bacci's work, and the experiments were carried out in controlled conditions, but the results were the same, even when the radio was isolated inside a Faraday cage, which blocks all external radio and electrical signals.

Some in the paranormal field claim that in order to try to debunk the Bacci experiment, they have unplugged the radio, taken the back off to ensure there are no batteries present, and found that the voices persist even without power. This is not the case. Bacci's radio does require power at all times to operate. However, skeptics have removed all three vacuum tubes from the radio and found that the voices continue.

The Global Movement

As the EVP research movement grew, the American Association of Electronic Voice Phenomena, founded in 1972 by EVP researcher Sarah Estep. It later became known as the Association Transcommunication (ATransC) and survives to this day.

This was followed by research associations forming all around the world, starting with des Vereins für Transkommunikations-Forschung (German Association for Transcommunication Research), which was founded in Germany in 1975.

Estep began her research into EVP using a a reel-to-reel tape recorder in 1976 after reading about the work of Friedrich Jürgenson and Konstantin Raudive. She went on to become a leading researcher in her field, making hundreds, if not thousands, of recordings of voice messages, some of which she identified as deceased friends and relatives and even intelligences of extraterrestrial origin.

Perhaps Estep's best-known legacy is her popularisation of an EVP classification system. It was similar to a previous system of classification proposed by Raudive. Estep's system used the same A, B, and C classes, with "Class A" being used to categorise the highest-quality EVPs and "Class C" being the poorest examples.

In the 21st century, we've seen an explosion of ITC devices. Unlike their predecessors, the new versions are mass-produced and sold to any interested investigator. With the advent of smart phones, the technology has even become the basis of mobile phone apps.

The first of these devices was called a "Frank's Box," which was invented by Frank Sumption. His idea of a device that sweeps through radio frequencies has become commonplace in the paranormal field, more commonly known as a "spirit box" or "ghost box."

Advances in technology have also made it easier for paranormal investigators to capture EVPs while on ghost hunts. Gone are the days of investigators having to lug around large tape recorders. Now, handheld digital audio recorders make it easy to record and quickly review EVP sessions.

EVP Research Timeline

1910

Father Roberto Landell de Mour, a Brazilian Catholic priest and inventor, used a device that allowed two-way communication with spirits based on radio technology.

1920

American inventor Thomas Edison fuelled the possibility that technology could be used to communicate with spirits. In an interview, he said he was proposing giving investigators a more scientific approach to spiritualism than the other more "crude methods" employed at the time, but died in 1931 having never completed the device.

1932

Reverend Charles Drayton Thomas, a member of the Society for Psychical Research, captured a spirit voice in a recording while investigating the validity of a well known medium of the time, Gladys Osborne Leonard.

1940s

In 1941, Attila von Szalay used one of the first commercially available home recording devices to capture EVPs on a blank record. He worked with psychologist Raymond Bayless and became one of the first to experiment with a reel-to-reel tape recorder.

1952

Agostino Gemelli inadvertently captured a voice while attempting to record the sounds of Gregorian chants in Milan with Father Pellegrino Ernetti. They were experiencing technical issues with the microphone, causing Gemelli to looked to the heavens and ask his dead father for help. When they reviewed the tape, they heard a voice that Gemelli recognised as his dead father.

1959

Friedrich Jürgenson caught unexplained voices on tape while trying to record bird song in woodland. Later in his research, Jürgenson became the first to combine the technique of recording EVPs with the earlier method of radio contact in order to improve his results. Jürgenson went on to write two books on the subject of EVP, 'Voices from the Universe' and 'Voice Transmissions With The Deceased'.

1965

Konstantin Raudive initially worked with Juergenson to capture EVPs. In one of these early experiments Raudive heard multiple voices in various languages, one of which translated as "go to sleep, Margaret" - he took this as a reference to someone of the same name he knew who had recently passed. He later captured the voice of his mother using his childhood name.

Raudive used several methods of recording EVPs, each method was carried out in strict laboratory conditions and asked volunteers to interpret the voice to avoid bias. His methods included using:
- a normal microphone connected to a tape recorder
- a standard radio that was not tuned to any station
- a modified radio with a germanium diode fitted

1972

The American Association of Electronic Voice Phenomena was founded by Sarah Estep. It later became known as the Association Transcommunication (ATransC) and survives to this day.

1974

Marcello Bacci started public performances in Italy of his method of spirit communication, in which he used an old military radio and later a larger vacuum tube radio set. Audience members were given the chance to hear the voices of their deceased loved ones.

1976

Des Vereins für Transkommunikations-Forschung (German Association For Transcommunication Research) was founded.

1976

Sarah Estep began her research after reading about the work of Friedrich Jürgenson and Konstantin Raudive using a reel-to-reel tape recorder. She popularised the first widely-accepted A, B, C EVP classification system.

1982
George Meek and William O'Neil used a similar germanium diode to Raudive's to develop their Spiricom, a radio-base device which made two-way communication with the dead possible.

Choosing the Right Equipment

Even if you're not attempting to capture EVPs, an audio recorder is a very useful tool to have on a ghost hunt because it mimics the human sense of hearing. Since so many hauntings include reports of unexplained knocks and bangs, footsteps, disembodied voices, and other sounds, it makes sense to try to capture evidence of this.

A digital audio recorder is capable of recording for hours on end, allowing you to create an audio log of the investigation. Should you hear any strange sounds, knocking, or voices, you can play them back to review them.

If using audio to log the investigation, you should ensure that the recorder is running continuously. Audio files are relatively small compared to a modern memory card's capacity, which means you can easily record several hours of audio.

When you start recording, say the time out loud. This will then give you a timeframe for the whole recording. When moving around the property you're investigating, describe your movement out loud; for example, "we're moving into the living room."

It's also a good idea to note in the recording how many people are present in each situation or vigil. This means if a sound is captured in the recording, you'll know if you were in a room alone or not; this will tell you if the sound could have been caused by someone else present - perhaps a fellow investigator simply cleared their throat.

You should also note verbally any non-paranormal sounds that are heard during the investigation. This includes sounds from outside the property, people moving, objects being dropped, coughs, sneezes, and stomach rumbles. Even the sound of the recorder itself being moved across a surface can be hard to identify during playback without a frame of reference.

You might think you'll remember these sounds when you listen back, but things can often sound quite different when captured by the recorder.

Having a running commentary in the recording will enable you to eliminate these sounds from your investigation, leaving only the unexplained sounds to be investigated.

Digital vs. Analogue Recording

Normally, when debating digital versus analogue audio recording methods, digital is the clear winner. Mainly because old analogue devices increase the chance of noise in the recording, this could be in the form of unwanted hiss, pops and rumbling.

But when it comes to the paranormal, it's not so simple, and investigators get results using both methods. Of course, all the early pioneers in EVP research would have been using analogue devices.

A digital method of audio recording would be a modern handheld audio recorder or dictaphone, the audio recording app built into your mobile phone or tablet, or audio recording software on a laptop.

Analogue refers to devices that use a magnetic storage medium, such as a cassette recorder or reel-to-reel tape machine. Today, these devices are considered antiquated, but since these sorts of recording devices proved so popular in the early days of EVP research, perhaps they shouldn't be ignored now.

Because the mechanics of how a spirit voice can be transposed on to a recording is far from understood, we can't rule out that it could be easier for a spirit to speak via an analogue device. After all analogue devices capture raw audio in real-time on magnetic tape.

Whereas a digital audio recorder samples the audio in tiny slices, which are then encoded in a digital format, and saves them to a digital storage medium like a memory card or hard drive. Due to the fragmented way hard drives work, the audio may not even be written in a linear sequence on the drive.

So, logic dictates that analogue might be a better method to capture EVPs, although it does have some downsides. It comes at a higher cost as you'll have to buy tapes if you want to archive your work. There's no easy way to skip back and replay audio instantly or jump between recordings with a tape recorder; you have to use the old-fashioned rewind button.

Most paranormal investigators like the ability to transfer their audio files to a computer for analysis. This is easy with digital devices, as the audio file can be transferred in seconds. With an analogue device, the only way to transfer the audio is by using a sound capture device connected to your computer or laptop via USB. You'll then need to connect the tape recorder's output to the device. This type of transfer is done in real time, so if you recorded an hour of audio, it will take an hour to be re-recorded onto your computer.

This type of transfer is a destructive process, and if high-quality audio connectors aren't used, then noise and interference may be introduced into the recording.

Analogue cassette and tape recorders can be picked up on auction sites for very reasonable prices; everything from vintage reel-to-reel tape recorders to 90s cassette recorders to retro dictaphones that record to mini-cassettes is available. Before committing to buying one, you should ensure that you're able to easily and cheaply buy the tapes you'll need. Surprisingly, new and unused tapes are also available for most types of recorders.

Recommended Audio Recorders

The important thing to remember when choosing an audio recorder is that there is no such thing as a dedicated "EVP recorder." You don't need to buy a specialist device from a ghost hunting store; you just need a normal, off-the-shelf recorder.

There are countless makes and models of audio recorders available on websites like eBay, Amazon, or electrical stores.

The most popular devices are digital voice recorders, most often either Olympus or Sony, which range from about $75 up to $180. The lower-priced recorders in this range are great entry-level devices which have an outstanding battery life and in-built memory that will allow you to record for hours on end. Those at the higher end of this price range are used by many well-established paranormal investigators.

Most of these devices make it easy for you to skip backward and forward when you review a recording. Many of the Olympus models have a button that lets you jump back a few seconds. Some let you slow down playback at the touch of a button, making it easier to listen to any potential voices in your recordings.

However, there are plenty of much more basic recorders that start for as little as $20, and although cheap, many investigators get as good results from a cheap recorder as others do from much more expensive devices.

At the other end of the scale are Tascam and Zoom digital audio recorders. These are professional-level audio recorders that record extremely clean and clear audio. They're of such high quality that they are used by podcasters, radio professionals, and video producers.

Tascam tends to be a little bit cheaper than Zoom, but both are of similar quality thanks to their built-in dual omnidirectional condenser microphones. Omnidirectional microphones are better at picking up sounds no matter which direction they come from. Where as a directional microphone will only hear what is in front of it. Some dictaphones, especially smaller ones, may only use a directional mic to capture just the user's voice as they hold the device.

If you are using a high-end recorder, you may feel like you are capturing fewer EVPs, but the better sound quality is actually preventing you from misidentifying false positives because you can hear those sound events for what they actually are instead of incorrectly interpreting them as a potential EVP.

If you're not yet ready to fork out cash on an audio recorder, then use the one you already have in your pocket. Most smart phones have an audio recording or voice notes/memo app built in that is good enough for paranormal investigations.

If a suitable app isn't installed on your phone by default, then there are audio and voice recording apps available in the app stores. When selecting an app, you should avoid "EVP recorders" or audio apps aimed at ghost hunters, as these apps are likely to include unnecessary features and could even reduce the quality of your audio by applying needless effects and processing.

There is no right or wrong when it comes to choosing an audio recorder for EVPs; what works for one investigator doesn't work for everyone. If you get the opportunity, try out other people's recorders. Make sure they are comfortable to hold, feel solid, that the playback controls aren't too fiddly, and that the sound quality is good.

It's not even really about the price and quality. Some paranormal investigators believe that cheaper, poorer-quality devices could be better for capturing EVPs, although, as previously mentioned, this could be due to lower-quality audio causing false positives.

Later in the book, we will look at EVP classifications in detail. One classification is "Type 1" or "transformative EVP." These are voices captured in recordings where the speech is a manipulation of other dissimilar sounds.

Cheaper or lower-quality recording devices, such as analogue tape recorders, are much more prone to picking up background noise, hisses, hums, and low rumbles. Low-cost audio recorders often have in-built microphones that might not be sufficiently shielded to filter out the sounds of the inner workings of the recorder.

This might sound like a negative, but some believe these normally unwanted sounds might be crucial to the formation of transformative EVPs, as this classification of EVP is made up of background noise that has been transformed.

However, you can still use a high-quality recorder and research transformative EVPs by using a white noise generator or similar random sound or tone generator to introduce background noise into the recording in the hopes that it can be transformed into an EVP.

In addition to your recorder itself, you may also want to invest in one other piece of equipment: an external omnidirectional microphone. These won't be compatible with all recorders, but some models of handheld audio recorders will also have a standard 3.5 mm microphone jack, so you can plug one in.

The internal microphones in recorders are good, but they're not perfect. They are more likely to pick up noises from inside the recorder itself, especially in quiet environments. The built-in microphones are primarily designed to capture human speech, so their frequency range might be limited to the human frequency range. They also tend to be unidirectional so as to pick up the person speaking without background noise.

However, depending upon how much you spend, an external microphone can have a much better frequency sensitivity and can be omnidirectional, which means it picks up sounds coming at it from all directions.

Panasonic RR-DR60 Series Recorder

We covered recommendations, but there's one audio recorder that shouldn't be avoided despite what you might have heard about it. Some paranormal investigators call Panasonic's early dictaphone, the RR-DR60, "the most effective recorder in the world for capturing EVPs," but there are countless arguments stacked up against its effectiveness.

The Panasonic RR-DR60 IC Recorder was launched in the mid-1990s. It was one of the first digital audio recorders to hit the market, and because it was one of the first of its kind, it lacked a lot of the features that newer digital audio recorders have, most noticeably a USB connector and a removable memory card. This meant that the only way to get the audio off of the device was via its headphone jack, an uncommon 2.5 mm socket.

The thing that made the DR60 unique at the time was that it had a "voice activated system" (VAS) feature. This allowed the device to automatically pause recording when no sound was detected. This avoided blank portions in recordings.

This functionality is useful for those using the dictaphone for the purpose it was originally designed for - making voice memos and notes, but the reason paranormal investigators liked this recorder was because they could leave it in the voice-activated mode and call out to any spirits that might be present. They could then leave a gap and remain silent before moving on to the next question. When reviewing the audio, the silence between the questions would not have been recorded unless someone or something had made a noise. If a voice was heard answering the question, this was deemed to be an example of an EVP.

The VAS feature made the DR60 perfect for quick-fire EVP sessions where the investigator would record for a minute or two and then review the audio before continuing. The lack of drawn-out silent periods in the recording sped this up dramatically, and working in this way reduced the need to go through hours of audio after an investigation. It also meant that if an answer was heard as an EVP, the investigator could question the response further in their next quick-fire burst of questions.

The DR60's instruction manual doesn't list its frequency response; this is very unusual for an audio recording device and is probably due to the fact that its range is so poor. There have been varying results from those who have tested the device, but they generally agree that the upper limit of the DR60's frequency range is about 18 kHz, although most state the figure to be 15 kHz. The human ear can hear sounds up to around 20 kHz, so the

RR-DR60 doesn't outperform the human ear for high-frequency sounds as claimed.

At the low end of the scale, we can hear sounds from around 20 Hz, but it's claimed that the DR60 can record sounds as low as 4 Hz, although this seems very unlikely as this was a first-generation digital recorder that used a very basic audio codec that was first used in 1985. Based on this, the frequency response of the device could be much closer to that of a telephone call, which is optimised for voice only at around 300 to 3,400 Hz.

The Panasonic IC Recorder wasn't just troubled by a poor frequency response; it also had a very poor sample rate. The higher the sample rate, the crisper and clearer the audio sounds, but unfortunately for the DR60, it was only able to sample the sound six times per second. To put that into perspective, a compact disc contains music that is sampled 44,100 times per second.

When you take the Panasonic RR-DR60's poor frequency response and its truly awful sampling rate into account, you end up with very muffled and poor-quality recordings at the best of times, as you'd expect from a 20-year-old recorder. Then, when you switch on the voice activation feature, it cuts out the silence in between any sounds, leaving just the noisy parts of the recording bunched up together. This means that what could have started out as tiny but natural sounds spread out across a long recording ends up as a short but constant sound made up of these noises. This is made worse by the device's onboard noise reduction and auto-gain functions.

Essentially, the device creates short bursts of noise through poor audio processing, triggers itself to record, and these noises get distorted due to poor audio compression. The silence between the noises is ignored, so the noises become a more sustained sound.

The other problem with the silent parts of the recording being removed is that you'll have lost the chance to enhance the quieter parts of the audio in order to listen for lower volume EVPs, which might have been under the minimum threshold required to cause the device to start recording.

Computer Recording

In the same way that you can carry out research using a mobile phone, you can also use a computer, or more likely, a laptop. The good thing about recording on a laptop is that the audio is captured directly in the audio software that you will later use to analyse it.

The most commonly used software is a piece of free, open-source audio software called Audacity. Those who are more experienced working with audio might prefer to use Adobe Audition, which offers users many tools for creating, mixing, and editing audio.

Both Audacity and Audition are available for Windows and Apple Mac, and at their core, they both have a very similar waveform editor.

One of the advantages of using a computer to capture EVPs is that you can see the audio waveform appear on screen as you record. If a sound is captured that you didn't hear aloud, it will show up as a peak in the waveform, and you can then stop recording and instantly review it. Having a waveform available in real time makes it much quicker and easier to skim through and check for EVPs. Moments where an investigator is speaking and when the room falls silent can clearly be distinguished from the shape of the waveform.

Laptops are also good because they let you connect external devices via their standard 3.5 mm microphone jack or USB port. This means you can plug in external omnidirectional microphones. The USB connection allows for microphones to be powered, so you can use a condenser mic, which is much more sensitive and can generally pick up a wider frequency range than a normal unpowered dynamic microphone - the type you'd find in cheaper audio recorders, mobile phones, and the laptop itself.

The possibilities are really endless when you factor in external devices paired with a laptop. You can use radio mics to monitor or record audio from another room, or even use multi-track and multiple inputs to record the audio from several areas at once in one master recording file.

One thing to be aware of if using a laptop to capture EVPs is that the microphones in these sorts of devices are designed to primarily be used as part of a video call, so in most cases they will be tuned to pick up audio in the human vocal range that is close to the microphone while trying to exclude any background noise like the distant sound of people talking in another room.

The same is partially true for digital voice recorders; they too are tuned to be more sensitive to the human vocal range, but since one of their primary uses is to record lectures and group conversations, they will pick up more than just a voice immediately in front of the microphone.

Spirit Boxes

A spirit box is a popular paranormal gadget that scans through the radio spectrum in the hopes that spirits can make their voices heard amongst the white noise and fleeting snippets of radio broadcasts. Although it's sometimes forgotten, this too is a form of EVP and uses a principle similar to the work of one of the early pioneers of EVP, Marcello Bacci.

The idea of using what is essentially a modified radio to pick up the voices of the dead divides the paranormal community, with many thinking it is a valid way to communicate with spirits, while others think it is nothing more than random radio noise.

The box rapidly scans through the AM, MW, and FM radio spectrums, and as it does, fleeting bursts of white noise and static can be heard. Some spirit boxes have various settings that allow you to tweak which bands the device scans through and how much of each frequency step you hear; this usually ranges from a hundredth of a second up to a second or more.

It's believed that spirits are able to change or influence these bursts of audio in order to form sounds, words, or even sentences.

In order to use the device, you should call out to any spirits that might be present and ask them questions, then listen for their answers within the noise of the spirit box. Ideally, this should be a response that spans across several steps of the frequency scan.

Unless you are in a cave or well-shielded building, you will almost certainly hear fragments of speech and music from radio stations. Although this might include words, what you are listening for are meaningful words and intelligent responses to your questions.

Some paranormal researchers prefer to put their spirit box inside a small bag that acts as a Faraday cage. This filters out the entire electromagnetic spectrum, which means that radio broadcasts don't make it to the device. In this case, it is much more likely that any voice that is heard is a result of paranormal contact.

Laser Beam EVPs

Many paranormal investigators believe that ghosts and the electromagnetic spectrum are intrinsically linked, and since laser light is part of the EM spectrum, laser beams can be used to capture EVPs.

It's not uncommon to use a device called an EM pump as part of an investigation. The gadget pumps energy out into the environment around it in the hopes that spirits can draw on that energy and use it to manifest or communicate.

The obvious fact that is often overlooked is that you can pump electromagnetic energy into your surroundings using just about anything, from a flashlight to a fan heater; in fact, even the human body gives out electromagnetic energy in the form of heat.

Another source of EM energy, similar to a flashlight, is a laser. Light, including laser light, travels in waves of varying frequencies in much the same way as radio waves, which are also part of the same spectrum. Of course, radio waves are capable of transmitting data - everything from wifi and mobile phone data to FM radio broadcasts in the form of music and speech.

The radio wave portion of the electromagnetic spectrum is the ideal frequency range for sending audio because the energy kicked out by a radio transmitter travels so far, but just about any form of EM energy can transmit data, including laser light. In fact, before Bluetooth took over the world, wireless headphones that used an invisible infrared light source to transmit the music were common. They worked in much the same way as your television remote control, which sends invisible light signals that your TV can decode.

A visible laser, like the common red and green laser pens that can be bought commercially, can be modified to send an audio signal to a light-sensitive receiver. This means that audio can be wirelessly sent across a room, meanwhile pumping EM energy into the environment. This is where it gets really interesting for paranormal investigators. Specialist paranormal equipment manufacturers also produce EVP laser microphones for this purpose.

As a beam of audio-transmitting laser light passes through the air, paranormal researchers theorise that spirits may be able to manipulate or interfere with the light's waveform in order to change the sound being transmitted or even add a sound of their own into the stream, like a voice.

This allows an investigator to call out to any spirits that might be present and encourage them to respond. The investigator can then monitor the audio being carried by the laser in real time, which could include the spirit's responses.

The principle is basically the same as the idea behind a spirit box. However, in theory, it should be much easier for a spirit to manipulate a laser beam. The light is visible as it passes through the air, so if a spirit can see the environment around it, then it will be able to see where it can interact with the laser, whereas radio waves are invisible, presumably even to ghosts.

Secondly, the laser transmission system relies on line of sight; it can't pick up signals from outside the building or even the room. This eliminates the possibility that external broadcasts could be interfering and giving false-positive results.

EVPs via Telephone Calls

This method of EVP research is often called the Phone Experiment. This is a real-time method of listening to EVPs while using a telephone. The idea isn't a new one. One of the early pioneers in EVP, Sarah Estep, once recorded a telephone call from a fellow EVP researcher, Konstantin Raudive, who had died 20 years previously.

The idea of hearing the voices of the dead over a telephone has been adapted by modern-day paranormal investigators using modern technology.

During a paranormal investigation, a mobile phone is used to call the phone of another investigator. It is then put into speakerphone mode and placed in an isolated part of the location being investigated.

The investigators then go to another room with the second phone and call out to the spirits, asking questions and encouraging them to answer while listening for responses through the receiving phone.

Sometimes one investigator remains in the room with the first phone and calls out in the same fashion while the other investigators listen in from the other room.

The exact science of how this process might work is unknown, but it's easier to imagine how it could have worked in the days of Sarah Estep when phone lines carried analogue signals that were susceptible to interference and cross-lines were a common issue. It's conceivable that an intelligent spirit could use its energy to imprint its thoughts on a phone call.

Today, all telecoms, including landline calls, are digitally encoded, which suggests that a spirit would need a degree in computer science to manipulate audio. Since the advent of digital telecoms, interference and cross-lines are a thing of the past.

However, since it seems that spirits are able to communicate using other digital devices, such as handheld audio recorders, there must be a way that they can do so with modern phones too. Presumably the spirit is able to imprint its voice using the analogue component of the device - its microphone. Microphones work using electromagnetic induction created when a diaphragm is vibrated by sound waves. Ghosts are said to be intrinsically linked with electromagnetism, so the theory might fit.

It shouldn't be forgotten that when you make a call on your phone, the signal is sent to a nearby mobile phone tower, bounced around your mobile phone provider's network infrastructure, passed over to the receiving phone's provider, sent to a cell tower, and then received by the second phone. So, if you are monitoring audio from a phone in the next room, that signal is actually travelling a very long way before you hear it.

So why not cut out the middleman? A cheap pair of walkie-talkies placed in different rooms would give you exactly the same result. One walkie-talkie transmits audio, while the walkie-talkie in the room you are in receives that signal. A direct line of communication.

Walkie-talkies are a little more prone to external interference, but because they are locked to one frequency and have limited power, distant transmissions wouldn't carry far enough to interfere in most cases.

You could also experiment with transmitting trigger sounds through the walkie-talkies and the phone line. This would mean that not only does the trigger sound play aloud in the room, but it would also permeate the entire room and beyond in the form of electromagnetic waves. Trigger sounds could be anything from the sound of a battle when investigating a former battlefield to the sound of prison guards jangling their keys in a former jail. These triggers are another way to encourage spirits to respond.

How to Capture EVPs

Today, EVP experiments are more commonly associated with ghost hunts in the field, but at the beginning of the 20th century, the early pioneers of EVP research proved that you can conduct EVP experiments just about anywhere. Much of their research was carried out as part of early séances, which would take place at the medium's home or performance space. The medium's job was to pull the spirits through and communicate with them.

For more than a century, EVP was a field of research that was conducted in homes, laboratories, offices, and workshops. It was only in the early 2000s, when television ghost hunting programmes started using the technique during their investigations, that it switched to being something that is more commonly done at a haunted location.

For example, the 100,000 audio tapes of EVPs recorded by Konstantin Raudive were made without the need to visit a haunted location. Raudive used several methods of recording EVPs, each method was carried out in strict laboratory conditions, which included screening from external radio interference. The same is true of Marcello Bacci, who worked out of a small performance space in Grosseto, Italy. Sarah Estep conducted her EVP research at home, where she had a dedicated space that housed various types of recording equipment.

One of the advantages of practicing EVP recording at home or a controlled location is that you're able to experiment with various types of equipment without having to lug kit around to haunted locations, where you might not be able to plug electrical equipment in and can't always guarantee silence. It's a great way to start experimenting with older, less portable devices like vintage reel-to-reel tape recorders or radio receivers. Remember, both Raudive and Bacci received their voices through unmodified vacuum radios tuned to a part of the frequency band where there was no station, so that it just produced white noise.

Where do the voices come from if you're not in a haunted location? In the case of Sarah Estep, it was often the voices of deceased friends and family members that came through in her recordings. Similarly, in Marcello Bacci's performances, it was the deceased loved ones of audience members who made contact.

So, even if your home isn't haunted, you can still invite spirits to communicate with you there, including those of a particular person, such as a deceased loved one, with whom you wish to make contact. If recording EVPs at home, you should try to conduct your sessions at a regular time in the hopes that spirits may learn that there will be an opportunity to come back and communicate again.

Wherever you are recording, it's a good idea to make a recording of the ambient sounds at the location before you begin your investigation. While recording this, make sure the building is empty if possible and quiet, and record for around half an hour. This will give you a baseline or reference audio recording, which you can refer to later when analysing your session audio.

Setting Up Your Equipment

The first and most important thing to do is read your device's instruction manual and familiarise yourself with the recorder's functions and features, especially any that might be detrimental to the device's ability to pick up EVPs.

No matter what make and model of audio device you are using, you should avoid any noise-canceling or low-cut features, as these will automatically boost, alter, and manipulate the audio you are recording. It's a great feature if you're using the device for its intended purpose as a voice recorder, but not so much when researching EVPs.

You may also find that your device has an auto-gain feature turned on by default. This feature will automatically adjust the sensitivity of the microphone. If you shout into the recorder, it will dip the microphone to accommodate, but when recording in a silent situation, it will boost the gain on the microphone, pushing it to its most sensitive setting.

This is great as it means you will hear really quiet sounds, but it will also mean that something that sounds very loud might have actually been very quiet if the audio hadn't been automatically boosted. So if you keep this feature turned on, you shouldn't assume that sounds in the recording are as loud as they appear to be.

Automatic gain can also mean that the struggling microphone amplifies the ambient sound so much that the recording consists of a lot of background noise in the form of hiss or low-end rumbling. In the same way that unwanted visual artefacts in a photograph or video can cause us to see things that aren't really there, unwanted noise in an audio recording can also lead to audio pareidolia. This is when the human brain tries to find patterns and familiar sounds in the chaos and misinterprets random sounds as voices.

Be sure to set your device to record in the highest possible recording quality; this is usually a WAV PCM format rather than the heavily compressed MP3 format.

If you can change the sample rate, then use at least 44,100 Hz. Always choose the high-quality (HQ) or "lossless" setting, or if available on your device, extra high-quality (XHQ) or super high (SHQ). Avoid long play (LP), as this mode extends the recorder's storage by drastically reducing the audio quality so that the file size is smaller.

Some recorders will have a setting for the microphone's sensitivity level. This may give you a sliding scale of sensitivity or the option of low, medium, or high. You may need to experiment with these options to determine which is most suitable for a paranormal investigation. Usually a higher sensitivity is desirable because you'll want to be able to hear everything going on in the room as this adds important context to your recordings, but too high and you might pick up too much background noise.

It might also be a good idea to use a windshield or muffler, which helps reduce unwanted noise from the wind or breeze. A suitable shield can be bought for more professional recorders, like those in Tascam's and Zoom's ranges.

If recording with a mobile device, look for the recording quality settings in the app and set the recording quality to the highest setting, ideally lossless quality. Where possible, switch from MP3 to WAV.

Recording with a computer makes things much easier as you can set the session to a high quality. The settings are defined up front, and the raw audio is recorded as a waveform. It's only when you save the recording that you need to specify a file format, and again, you should save the recording as a WAV file rather than an MP3.

Don't forget the golden rule: always use fresh batteries. Before every investigation, put brand new batteries in your recorder or make sure it is fully charged. Not only do you want to avoid the batteries running out while you're recording, but low batteries may also result in a reduction in the quality of the recording or unwanted noise.

Ensuring High-Quality Recordings

Now that you're ready to start capturing EVPs, you're going to need to make sure they're of the best possible quality; this will make it much easier to analyse them later.

The first step towards achieving crystal-clear EVPs is to ensure the environment is free of background noise. So turn off the heating, air conditioning, fans, and any other loud mechanical devices that could spring into action. Make sure that windows and internal and external doors are closed to reduce noise bleeding through from other parts of the building or from outside.

Place your recorder away from other electrical devices to avoid unwanted interference, especially any device that transmits a radio signal of any kind.

Limit the number of people in the building or room during the EVP session. For every additional person present, there's the added possibility that a strange noise captured isn't paranormal and is just a human moving; this can be very hard to debunk retrospectively during playback and analysis.

Place the audio recorder on a flat, solid surface. Holding a device is a common cause of unexpected sounds, as the slightest change in pressure in your grip can cause the plastic housing of the device to flex and make a sound. This is especially true of recorders with in-built microphones. This sound is often inaudible at the time but can sound very loud inside the device where its microphone is housed.

If holding your recorder is unavoidable then use a firm grip and avoid moving your hand while recording.

Avoid placing the recorder on the floor, as any movement could cause vibrations, resulting in the device translating the vibration as a sound or causing the recorder itself to rock slightly, causing a noise.

Do not place the recorder inside of anything, such as a box, pouch, or your pocket, as this will severely limit the device's sensitivity or make sounds muffled and impossible to either debunk or identify as genuine EVPs.

Take a seat, if possible, and get comfortable. You should also try to stay as still as possible during the session to avoid making any unnecessary noise. Where possible, remove any clothing, like heavy jackets that might rustle or heavy, clanging jewellery. Not only could these sounds be misidentified as paranormal contact in the recording later during playback and analysis, but you could also drown out genuine EVPs.

With the basics in place, the next few best-practice tips are essential.

Upon pressing record, leave five to 10 seconds of silence at the beginning to allow the recorder to adjust to the baseline noise level. If you're using a tape recorder, then remember that cassettes have a seven to 10 second buffer at the beginning that can't be recorded on, so allow for this.

Introducing each recording is very important when it comes to analysing your audio later; it means you will know exactly what you are listening to.

At the start of each recording, you should start by speaking out loud the date, time, location, and number of people present. You can also give the recording a number, e.g., "EVP recording number one." This will make it easier to keep track of recordings when you review the audio later. Knowing where the audio was captured and who was present will help you debunk sounds heard in the recording. To help you debunk non-paranormal noises, you should note verbally any sounds that are heard during the session so that you can eliminate them from your investigation when you later review the audio.

For example, if you cough, sneeze, clear your throat, move slightly, or your stomach rumbles, say out loud "that was me" so that there is no doubt later. It's surprising how different some normal noises can sound with no context in a recording and how they can be very hard to identify, which could lead you to a false paranormal conclusion.

Do not whisper during a session. If you have something to say, say it out loud. Whispers can be very hard to identify later when you review the audio.

How long you record for is really up to you, but a good duration for a session would be around 10 to 20 minutes. You want to give the experiment the best chance of success, but recording too much will mean you have a lot of audio to listen back to later.

However, there are a few different methods that determine the recording time. We'll look at these next.

Active vs. Passive EVP Sessions

When it comes to recording, there are a few different tried and tested methods available. We'll look at realtime and burst recordings later in the chapter, but first let's look at the differences between active and passive recording sessions.

Passive EVP Sessions

A passive EVP session is one in which the investigators conducting the experiment are not actively asking questions or encouraging the spirits to interact. The method was pioneered by Konstantin Raudive and involves no human interaction.

In its simplest form, it involves setting up a recording device in a room or enclosed area, leaving the area, and leaving the recorder running in silence. The idea behind this is that a supernatural entity may inadvertently make a sound in the recording.

Passive sessions might be a better option for locations that are said to house a residual haunting where intelligent two-way communication may not be possible.

After 20 minutes, or however long you feel is necessary, you can retrieve the recorder and review the audio to see if you've captured any unexplained sounds or voices during the session.

We previously discussed steps that should be taken to minimise and eliminate external noise. When conducting a passive EVP experiment, this is more important than ever as you won't be in the room and won't be able to note any non-paranormal sounds heard to eliminate them from your investigation when you review the audio.

Care should be taken to ensure all doors and windows are closed and that adjoining rooms are silent too.

In a silent setting, the device may overcompensate with audio gain and amplification, which could mean that even distant voices in other rooms and floors of the building are picked up.

Although the recorder is normally left in a quiet environment, this isn't always necessary. The device could be left recording in an allegedly haunted location during normal daily life to see if anything is captured. This would still be classed as a passive session, as there are no direct or intentional attempts to actively communicate.

Active EVP Sessions

An active EVP session is when investigators are actively making attempts to communicate during the session. This normally involves asking a question out loud, such as "Is there anybody here?" Then leaving a few seconds of silence before the next question in the hopes that a response will be captured in the gap.

You could also sit in the room with the recorder and have a conversation with your fellow investigators to see if this encourages any spirit interaction. Although this isn't a direct attempt at communication, since you are still encouraging the spirits to communicate, it would still be classified as an active session.

Some researchers have found that when this method of attempting to capture EVPs is used, the voices heard will reference the conversation taking place or reply to certain things that were said. Remember not to be too talkative; you still need to give the voices a chance to be heard over your chatter.

Real-time and Burst EVP Sessions

Both the real-time and burst methods can be used as part of an active or passive EVP session; however, they are most often used during an active session as this method allows investigators to be more responsive.

Burst Session

A burst session is almost like a quick-fire EVP session. It involves recording two or three minutes of audio using the same methods described previously. The audio is then reviewed straight away, allowing the investigator to hear any potential voices that have been captured in the recording.

Real-time Session

A real-time, or "listen live," session is where the investigator monitors the audio being captured in real-time. This can be done using some of the methods described previously, such as capturing EVPs via laser beams or by using telephone calls and walkie-talkies.

However, the easiest and most common way to conduct a real-time EVP session is by simply plugging a pair of headphones into your audio recorder and monitoring the sound. You may find that you are able to hear sounds through the headphones that you can't hear with your ear alone, but the effectiveness of this depends on the sensitivity of the microphone, the frequency response of the headphones, and the quality of the onboard microphone preamp and headphone amplifier.

Listening to live EVPs can also be done through devices like a spirit box or modified radios like those used by Konstantīns Raudive and Marcello Bacci.

With both burst and realtime sessions, the idea is to listen to EVPs as they occur, or in the case of burst recordings, a couple of minutes later, while the investigator is still in the same location and conditions.

This allows investigators to follow up on any words or phrases they hear in order to continue the conversation.

While these methods, especially burst recordings, tend to get good results, you should remember that listening to audio via headphones while on an investigation might not be ideal when it comes to picking up quieter, more subtle voices. Therefore, you should always fully review and analyse your full recordings after the investigation to uncover anything you might have missed. There will be more on analysing EVP recordings later.

How to Call Out During EVP Sessions

Unless you are conducting a passive EVP session, you'll need to ask any spirits that might be present questions; this is called "calling out" or "asking out." It involves speaking aloud in an attempt to encourage any spirits nearby to come forward, talk to you, and answer your questions in your recordings.

When calling out, be polite and respectful, and don't make demands. Be sure to leave plenty of time after each question to allow the spirit time to answer. You may not hear anything at the time, but when reviewing the audio, EVPs could be present, and you'll be able to hear the spirit answering your question.

1. Leave a gap

When trying to capture EVPs, the single most important thing to remember is to remain silent and leave a space after your question to allow the spirit time to answer. It is in this silence that you will hopefully hear a reply in the form of an EVP. Leaving a gap of 20 seconds between questions is good practice.

2. Encourage, don't demand

You need to get the spirits on your side. If you're on a ghost hunt, then you're probably in the spirit's former home or a place that means something to that person, so treat them with respect. Tell them you're not there to mock them, that you want to communicate.

Chances are, you're not the first paranormal investigator on their patch. They might have been asked the same questions countless times before. If spirits truly do exist, then it's unlikely that they're going to be happy existing in spirit form for no purpose other than to amuse you.

Instead, ask the spirits if they need help or have a message. Show an interest in them, perhaps even to help them move on.

3. Make your questions relevant

When calling out to spirits, remember that they are unlikely to be from your time. Saying "please speak clearly into the laptop" would mean nothing to a 17th-century spirit. Instead, encourage the spirit to speak to you or into "the device with the red light on it"; make it as easy as possible for the spirit to understand by pointing and showing them where to talk.

Avoid words like "entity," "spirit," and "presence," as this is ghost hunter jargon and is also unlikely to be very clear to a 200-year-old ghost. Besides, ghosts may not realise they're dead, so if you call them a ghost, spirit, entity, or whatever else, they might just stand there watching and wondering who you are talking to.

Refer to the spirits as people: "Is there anyone here with us? Can you tell me your name?" Give that person, that consciousness, the confidence to step forward and communicate, give them a reason to reach out to you. Treating a spirit with respect and not as a "presence" or a thing will help with this.

Below is a list of example questions and phrases that you can use to try to encourage the spirits to communicate with you. You shouldn't copy these exactly; it is better to be yourself and talk in a natural and open way as you normally would.

If you can hear me, can you tell me your name?
Can you tell me something about yourself?
If you're here, can you let us know?
How many of you are with us right now?
My name is XXX, can you tell me your name?
Tell us who you are, introduce yourself, please.
Can you come and talk to us?
Why are you here?

Of course, if you establish a dialogue with a spirit, you can ask more in-depth questions, perhaps to establish how the spirit died or to confirm their identity. Try to ask questions that no one in the room would know the answers to so you can rule out fakery or people subconsciously affecting the outcome.

White Noise Generators

Radio noise is something that crops up often in the field of paranormal research, most often referred to as "white noise." However, white noise is actually just one specific type of radio noise that is characterised by its equal intensity at different frequencies, giving it a constant intensity across all audible frequency ranges.

It is referred to as "white" noise because the random electrical interference that creates it is spread across the whole audio spectrum of frequencies. In the same way that white light is made up of colours of all frequencies, white noise is made up of sounds of all frequencies. These random bursts of varying frequencies have an overall intensity that is constant.

Based on the theory that spirits can reorganise radio noise to form words, some EVP researchers use a white noise source to give spirits a base of raw sound to use to form words. This is done by playing back a pre-recorded sample of white noise, by recording near a source of static noise like a television or radio, or by using a white noise signal generator to artificially produce random and constant white noise.

The drawback to using this technique is that the white noise contaminates the recording, making it hard to analyse the audio. However, some EVP experts use audio editing software like Adobe Audition and Audacity or bespoke audio filtering software to remove the white noise, leaving only the more sustained sound in the recording, which could include spirit voices.

If using a source of white noise during an EVP session, be sure not to have the volume too high as it might flood your recording. Because white noise, by its very nature, covers the whole spectrum of sound, it will mask all other frequencies if it is too loud, including human speech and EVPs.

When it comes to filtering out the white noise from your recording, this can't be totally removed for the same reason. Again, because white noise, by definition, lives all across the frequency spectrum, audio filters can't distinguish it from the sounds you want to keep in your recording.

However, the good news is that you don't have to completely remove it. For the most part, your brain can't hear noise when it is masked by a real sound in the same frequency range. So the noise reduction techniques mentioned later in the book also apply to recordings where white noise is present.

Putting white noise aside for a moment, other types of radio noise are made up of a combination of three main sources:

Radio Frequency Interference (RFI)

Manmade radio frequency interference from electrical switches, motors, vehicle ignition systems, computers, and other electrical devices is picked up by the receiver's antenna. These noises are often referred to as "static."

Thermal Noise

Thermal noise is present in the receiver's input circuits, caused by the random thermal motion of molecules.

Atmospheric Noise

Atmospheric noise is created by electrical processes in the atmosphere. Primarily, this is caused by lightning discharges in thunderstorms. On a worldwide scale, 3.5 million lightning flashes occur daily (about 40 lightning flashes per second). The sum of all these lightning flashes results in atmospheric noise.

As well as white noise, some researchers add noise by using a fan or running water; these can be recordings or recordings of crowd babble, word fragments, or other constant ambient sounds.

The Ghost Frequency

In 1980, Vic Tandy was an experimental officer and part-time lecturer in the school of international studies and law at Coventry University in the UK. He was working alone late one night in a lab, which has a reputation for being haunted. He reported feeling anxious and claimed he could see dark objects out of the corner of his eye, but when he turned to face the greyish blob, there was nothing there.

The next day, the researcher noticed what some might describe as poltergeist activity. He was working on his fencing sword, which is made of a lightweight, flexible metal. He had the handle of the foil held in a vice on his desk when he noticed that the blade started vibrating, even though nothing was touching it.

Tandy realised that it was a specific frequency of infrasound in his lab that was being produced by a fan that was causing his discomfort and even the movement of the foil.

In 2003, an experiment using infrasound was carried out in London. Infrasound was played during a concert in the Purcell Room. Afterwards, the audience was interviewed and their responses were analysed by psychologists. On average, infrasound boosted the number of strange experiences by around 22% and caused the concertgoers to report feelings of sorrow, coldness, and anxiety.

The specific frequency of sound that Tandy detected in his lab was 18.98 Hz, and it is known to paranormal investigators as the "ghost frequency" or "ghost tone." The tone is impossible to hear as it falls just outside the range that the human ear can pick up.

While some parapsychologists think that the ghost tone tricks your senses into seeing, hearing, and feeling the type of unusual things that are commonly associated with hauntings, some EVP researchers believe that playing the ghost tone during an investigation increases the chances of capturing EVPs as the sound acts as a carrier wave or effective source of sound for transformation to occur.

If you'd like to experiment with playing the ghost tone during an investigation, you'll need to first use an audio tone generator website, which will allow you to play a clean tone at exactly 18.98 Hz. The problem is that most speakers can't actually reproduce this tone. Laptop speakers aren't very good at reproducing sounds under 300 Hz, and smartphone speakers are even worse.

There's no way to know if a sound you can't hear is playing, but the best way to ensure you are exposing yourself or your investigation to the frequency is to use a subwoofer with a large amplifier, the type you use as part of a home cinema system.

Regular speakers are optimised to reproduce sound waves at the peak of the human ear's frequency range; tones that are much higher or lower than this tend to be much weaker. However, subwoofers are designed specifically to play very low-frequency sounds, known in the movie industry as LFE, or low-frequency effects. The LFE sounds are amplified much higher to compensate for the low frequency.

You still won't be able to actually hear 18.98 Hz, but if you place your hand in front of the subwoofer, you will almost certainly be able to feel it, and that's exactly what is required for this experiment. It doesn't matter that you can't hear the sound; the vibration of the sound waves is said to affect your whole body and even your visual system.

Analysing EVPs

When it comes to EVP research, playback is arguably the most important and time-consuming task. It can also be quite tedious, but without a proper review of your audio, the whole EVP session is pointless.

Even if you were conducting a "quick fire" burst session or a "listen live" session and you reviewed the audio as you went during the session, you should still review all of the audio in full after the session.

The built-in speakers on audio recorders are often inadequate for a proper review, and while at a location, you may find it hard to find somewhere quiet enough to properly review the audio.

The simplest approach for reviewing and analysing your recordings is to plug your audio recorder directly into a good-quality external speaker or connect a pair of good-quality over-ear headphones. Either of these methods is really the minimum required effort; they're not ideal, but they're a good place to start.

A better approach is to transfer the audio to your computer; this allows you to review the audio in greater detail. Once on your computer, it then becomes easier to turn up the volume, pause, and go back to re-listen to specific parts of the recording again. Transferring audio is normally done via a USB lead, and audio files are compatible with Windows or Apple devices. You should refer to the specific instructions in your audio recorder's instruction manual for more details on this.

There are some cases where the process of transferring audio may be a little different and require a little more effort. If you're using an analogue recording device, such as an old tape recorder or an early dictaphone, then there won't be a USB port on the device. You may need some special audio leads and a USB audio interface in order to capture the audio. The downside of this is that the audio isn't transferred instantly like it is over USB; it is captured by the computer in real time, and poor-quality audio connections might lead to unwanted noise in the transferred audio.

Unfortunately, this is unavoidable and is the nature of analogue recordings. To ensure you obtain the best audio possible when transferring from analogue device, practice the transfer process in order to familiarise yourself with the ideal settings and levels required on both the recording device and the computer.

Once the audio is on your computer, you should again ensure you are listening to it through high-quality speakers, or better yet, a good pair of over-ear headphones.

MP3 and WAV files can be played easily on computers, either using Windows Media Player on a Windows machine or QuickTime Player on an Apple Mac. You can also use a free audio player such as VLC, which is available for both operating systems.

Listen to the audio from start to finish, from the moment you press record to the moment you press stop. EVPs don't always happen on demand, so you might hear unexpected voices in parts of the recording where you weren't actively asking for responses.

You should listen carefully for anything that sounds like a voice in the audio. If you hear anything, either make a note of the time in the recording or what you think the voice is saying. Or better still, isolate the specific piece of audio and save it as a separate file. This can be done using free audio editing software like Audacity or the more professional Adobe Audition.

When saving a highlight, be sure to leave a few seconds before and after the sound, as this provides important context should you wish to play these highlights to someone.

Be sure to set up a method of saving your sessions and recordings so that you can easily refer back to the raw session and find examples of the EVPs you captured. Of course, how you do this is up to you, but a good way to manage this is to create a folder with a meaningful name that includes a date code, such as "2021-10-31 - Hampton Castle." Save the raw audio recordings from your recording in this folder. Don't edit your raw recording files; this is your evidence. Editing the file could remove vital context, making later analysis impossible.

If you are logging the EVPs, then save a text-based log file document in the same folder and note anything you hear. So for example, if you hear a voice at 5:12 in the recording that sounds like it's saying "help me", then in the document type "05:12 - Help me".

You should use the same naming approach if you are isolating and saving the individual EVP clips. Again save the clips in the same folder and call the file "05-12 - help me.wav". This will allow you to easily find a specific EVP you captured and also tell you where you can find that EVP in the original recording.

The trickiest part can be hearing the voices, figuring out what they're saying, and recognising when something that sounds like a voice isn't a voice at all but has another explanation.

The problem is that when you listen back to audio alone, you don't have any real record of the causes of background noises and other sources of sounds other than your recollection of events. Your memory alone simply isn't reliable enough. You won't remember every sound that was heard at the time of recording; you may not have even picked up on the sound or been consciously aware of it.

Normally we are able to see the things around us in order to add context to help us understand what we're hearing, this is of course not the case with an audio recording.

If you are finding it hard to distinguish a sound from background noise, then your baseline recording might help. As mentioned previously, it's a good idea to make a recording of the ambient sounds at the location before you begin your investigation there. This is where that baseline reference recording might come in handy. If you hear a sound in your session recording, but you're not sure what's causing it, you can refer back to your baseline recording to see if it naturally occurred prior to the investigation during your baseline recording.

However, don't be too quick to rule out sounds heard in your baseline recording either, as the idea of creating a clean baseline recording as a reference contradicts the passive EVP session method, where researchers intentionally try to capture EVPs in silent environments. Both approaches are valid and should be researched.

While you're trying to pick out a sound from the background, don't ignore the background noise all together, as it provides important context and clues that may help you explain an unexplained sound in the recording. For example, if you hear a strange sound moments after someone takes a piece of electronic equipment out of their bag, that could be the piece of equipment being switched on.

Comparing the suspected EVP to the background noise can also give you an idea of how loud the sound was. Was it louder or quieter than the investigators' voices? Are there any other similarly pitched sounds heard before or after?

The quality of EVPs varies, and researchers need a certain amount of patience and concentration to distinguish them from background noise. Some words are difficult to understand, while others can be very clear.

Some EVP researchers liken understanding the voices in EVPs to learning a new language, but this isn't a good approach as it suggests that the words are unclear and the researcher is inventing ways to hear what isn't really there.

Auditory Pareidolia

As a paranormal investigator, you've probably come across the term "pareidolia" before. This is the tendency for the human brain to perceive a familiar or meaningful image in an object or pattern where, in fact, there is none. This becomes most relevant in ghost hunting when investigators see what looks like phantom faces in a blurry photo, which in reality aren't paranormal at all; it's just our minds seeing something that's not really there.

Pareidolia is a form of apophenia, which is a more general term for the human tendency to seek patterns in random information, and this applies to audio too. Just like with vision, we are all susceptible to hearing words that are not actually in the sounds we are hearing. This can occur by misinterpreting words that are being said or by hearing words in random noise.

Auditory pareidolia isn't the only thing that might cause you to misidentify an EVP. The truth is, understanding or interpreting what an EVP is saying is subjective. You will find that people often disagree with your interpretation of a word or phrase and hear something completely different. As the listener, you may be influenced by the question that was asked prior to the EVP or by your knowledge of the location you were investigating. You are likely to simply hear what you expect to hear.

Auditory pareidolia is by far the biggest and strongest argument against the credibility of EVPs. Skeptics maintain that the majority of EVP recordings are sounds that are misinterpreted; most often, they are caused by natural phenomena, including ambient sounds, atmospheric electrical interference, radio interference, faulty equipment, sounds caused by the recording device being moved or handled, or the sounds of the inner workings of the recorder itself. Because of this, you should do all that you can to validate your recordings.

Luckily, there are ways to remove subjectivity and validate your EVPs. First off, if you hear something anomalous, isolate the clip and remove all context by removing anything said around it or any questions asked. Then forget about it for a day or two. After this time, listen to the clip out-of-context and decide whether the sound still sounds like the word you thought it did previously, a different word, or nothing at all.

The next step is to get other people to listen to it, ideally a group who are not interested in the paranormal or familiar with EVP research. Again, make sure there is no context, and do not tell them what you believe the voice is saying. Don't tell the listener where the clip was recorded or what was being asked; just play them the sound and ask them to tell you what they hear.

If their interpretation matches yours, then this is good validation of the EVP. However, after asking several people you may find that the majority hear a different word or phrase to you. Since all these people heard the same speech without the influence of the context of the recording, this should tell you that your interpretation is wrong.

It's really important to remove the context when you review the audio after some time away from it and when asking others to review it. If a question was asked in the recording, then the listener may try to interpret the sound in a way that fits the question rather than listening objectively.

The Cocktail Party Effect

One of the benefits of using an audio recorder during an investigation is that it gives you another chance to hear something you might have missed at the time. Have you ever been on an investigation and someone has asked, "Did you hear that sound?" As soon as they mention it, you recall it, but at the time you weren't consciously aware of it. This is due to the "cocktail party effect."

The effect describes an ability of the human brain that allows us to focus our auditory attention on one particular stimulus while filtering out a range of other stimuli. This is most obvious at a party when you are able to hold a conversation with a single person while other partygoers chatter all around you.

It's for this reason that you might be listening to someone call out on a vigil and perhaps even waiting for responses through a spirit box or other gadget, and because your auditory attention is focussed on this, you might not notice normal or paranormal sounds coming from around you.

Let's go back to the cocktail party. After your chat, you might wander off and help yourself to a drink, ignoring the buzz of chattering guests, until you hear your name mentioned. Even though you weren't consciously aware of anything else that was being said, clearly you are hearing what's going on around you; your brain just filters it out unless it's relevant.

We may not remember hearing a disembodied voice or an unexplained sound during a vigil, but that's not a reason to assume it wasn't audible at all if the noise is later heard while playing back an audio recording. An audio recorder captures everything it hears within its frequency response, depending on its microphone sensitivity. If a sound is captured in a recording, it's not necessarily paranormal in nature just because you don't remember hearing it at the time.

Should You Enhance Recordings?

One area of EVP research that is often debated is whether the audio captured should be enhanced and manipulated or not. A researcher may choose to enhance their audio in order to make the words heard clearer or to filter out background noises.

The problem with doing this is that if you are intentionally manipulating the audio to make it sound more like the words you think it sounds like, then what you're left with is your ideal interpretation of your own subjective perception of what that EVP should sound like, not a true representation of what it sounded like at the time it was captured.

It's the audio equivalent of distorting a photo or video until it looks like what you want it to look like. Case in point: you could also manipulate the audio to sound less like words, which would also be an untrue representation of the sound.

EVP recordings often have a lot of hiss due to the nature of how they're recorded in very quiet situations. This hiss is similar to white noise, a cacophony of random sounds spanning across the whole frequency range. When this sound is run through a digital filter to clean it up, normally the high-frequency sounds are taken out. These are the frequencies that our ears are most sensitive to, therefore creating the dominant hiss sound in white noise.

What you're left with is a collection of sounds within a certain frequency range; this can sound very different, and with some of the noise removed, random patterns may present themselves, causing a greater risk of pareidolia.

Some EVP researchers sometimes capture what sounds like words spoken at a slower or faster speed than normal. It's not uncommon to use audio editing software to speed up or slow down recordings for this reason, but again, this should be avoided as changing the speed will cause the audio to become an inaccurate reproduction of the original sound.

Therefore, the filtering or manipulation of clips should be minimised and clips presented as close to their original form as possible. However, if done properly, manipulation can improve the audio. You can filter out just the extraneous sounds, leaving you with a more accurate representation of the captured sound.

There are also types of manipulation and enhancement that are acceptable and can be very useful when reviewing your audio, and that's the simple amplification of the audio in order to enable you to hear any potential EVPs more clearly.

While logic states that a clean recording is always preferable, many prominent investigators have established a trend of manipulating and enhancing their recordings. They often say that it makes it easier for the listener to hear the EVP, but of course, as mentioned previously, what's being heard may not be a true reflection of what was originally recorded.

Although it is generally not advised, there is no right or wrong when it comes to paranormal investigation, and what works for one investigator doesn't necessarily work for another. So, if you strongly feel the need to aggressively enhance your recordings, then do so with the awareness that you might be destructively altering your evidence.

In the spirit of keeping your audio as true to the source recording as possible, if you really must enhance it, then limit yourself to just one or two enhancements.

Of course, recording conditions vary, but try to find filters and enhancements that work for you and stick to them; at least this way, you'll be treating all potential evidence fairly. If you apply different filters to varying degrees on different clips, then you will not be able to make objective comparisons between the audio clips.

If there is a need for different filters or enhancements with different pieces of audio, then this merely highlights the problem with enhancement. It shows that you are intentionally altering a clip in order to make a noise sound more like the voice that you subjectively think it should sound like.

Enhance and Filtering Recordings

Before you do anything to your recordings, make sure you make a copy of the original files and back them up to ensure that you don't unintentionally and irreparably alter the original.

In order to enhance your audio, you'll need some audio editing software. The most commonly used are Audacity, Adobe Audition, both of which are available for Apple Mac and Windows computers, as well as Goldwave on Windows. Audacity isn't quite as good as Audition, but it is completely free to download and use.

Although these and other applications are great for editing audio, they're not really fit for the purpose of enhancing EVPs to the degree that some investigators push them. In the field of audio recording, there is a commonly used term, "signal to noise ratio." The "signal" is the audio you want, the voice, the music, or in this case, the EVP. The "noise" is any unwanted hiss, rumble, or buzz. So a high signal-to-noise ratio means there's lots of what you want to hear without much unwanted noise. This is the type of recording that audio editing software is designed to work with and what most audio industry professionals want to use the software for.

Unfortunately, in the case of EVP recordings, there's often a low or even negative signal-to-noise ratio, which means that the signal power is lower than the noise power. Editing software struggles to deal with this sort of audio because there is often not enough clean signal to successfully be restored. So, enhancing a very faint sound from a recording with significant ambient noise will often be too much of a stretch.

The problem is that the normal noise reduction or hiss removal tools in the software will not be able to tell the difference between the noise and your EVP, so when the filter is applied, it will either mute the whole recording or try to aggressively enhance a certain frequency range while softening the surrounding frequencies that it judges to be unwanted.

For their intended purpose, these filters work well. If you're trying to remove an unwanted hiss from a clean and loud recording of a speech, then the software will take away this hiss and leave the speaker's voice relatively untouched. However, when used to try to enhance faint sounds within a lot of noise, it may change them so significantly that the results are of no use as evidence.

Due to the nature of software, settings options and tools often change, so it would be impractical to offer step-by-step guides to enhancing audio in this book. Instead, we will take a look at the tools you can use, which should be similar to some extent across all audio editing software.

Some audio editing software allows you to switch to a "spectral frequency display" view rather than the standard waveform. This view can be very useful for identifying and removing or enhancing noise in your recordings. Don't worry if you're not familiar with working with audio frequencies and waveforms; there will be more on this later.

Amplification

Perhaps the most useful tool is amplify, which is normally found in the effects tools. This allows you to basically increase the volume of your clip. Be sure not to amplify your clip too heavily, as over-amplification will cause it to become distorted.

Start with a 1 to 3 dB (decibel) boost and play the audio to ensure it's not too loud. You will know if it is because the volume metre will be going into the red. If it's too loud, then press undo and try a lower level. If the audio is still too loud, don't simply apply another amplification on top; again, press undo to take you back to the original level and start with a slightly higher amplification. This will ensure your audio stays as clean and true to its original state as possible.

Although amplification is the best option for enhancing your clips and the least aggressive, it might not help in this case. The problem is, by trying to increase the volume of the EVP, what you're actually doing is increasing the volume of the whole clip, including the background noise. Since both elements get a boost, the EVP does not become any clearer. So another approach is to try to remove that background noise.

If you are using a spectral view of your recording, then after playing the sound through a few times, it may be easy to see where the sound is in the spectrum, not just in terms of when the sound starts and its duration, but also where it appears in the frequency range. If you are able to see the sound in the spectral view, then you can highlight and amplify it. This will more or less amplify just the selected sound without any of the unwanted noise.

Noise Reduction and Restoration
Most software has some basic noise reduction tool. This might be called simply "noise reduction," but also look out for restoration, hiss removal, hum removal, and vocal enhancers.

If you want to reduce the background noise, then noise reduction or restoration is your best option, but you could also try hiss removal. Vocal enhancer should be a last resort, as it is an automated tool that may struggle with clips with a lot of noise and apply filters too aggressively.

Experiment with the different settings, but, like with amplification, don't jump in with very harsh enhancements straight away. Try a less intense filter once, one with a low level of noise reduction. If this doesn't have much of an impact, or if you've applied too much, then again press undo to return to your unenhanced audio and start again with a different setting.

Capturing a Noise Print

In some applications, the noise reduction tool requires you to select a sample of noise for best results. The tool then subtracts this noise sample from the rest of the recording. If you made a baseline recording in this same environment, then you could use a portion of that recording as your noise print, or alternatively, use a quiet period in the recording before or after the suspected EVP appears.

You should try to pick a part of the recording where the noise is similar to the background sounds heard throughout the clip and at the point where the sound of interest is heard. Unfortunately, making the judgement is subjective. No two investigators would select the exact same area and this will cause results to vary.

Once you have highlighted the area of noise - ideally at least five seconds of audio, press the "capture noise print" option followed by the "process" button.

Understanding Frequencies and Waveforms

A major part of EVP research requires you to be able to analyse audio recorded during investigations. Knowledge of frequencies and waveforms will help you determine if a captured sound is a genuine EVP or just unwanted noise in your recording. The main terms you'll need to understand are frequency, amplitude, wavelength, and pitch. Knowledge of these key terms is vital when examining a waveform.

The best way to analyse an EVP is by using audio editing software such as Adobe Audition or Audacity. These applications allow you to view the waveform that represents that sound, zoom into it in order to pick out specific noises in the recordings, and amplify or enhance them. When looking at a waveform as a whole recording, it's hard to pick out anything useful, as the image above shows. However, it is clear to see areas of loud noise and silence.

Sound waves in a recording will normally be fluctuating vibrations consisting of many different frequencies and amplitudes, but to simplify things, we're going to introduce you to the parts of a uniform oscillating wave.

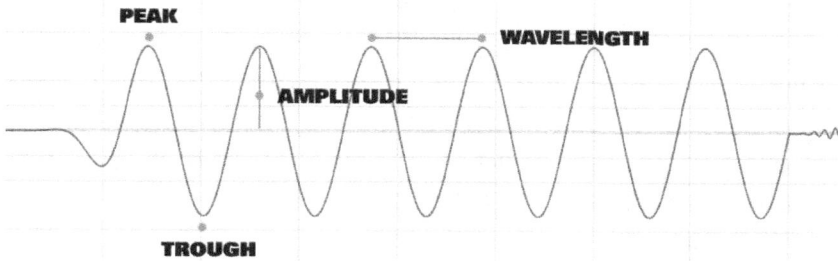

In the diagram above, you can see the important parts of a waveform, which you should understand in order to properly analyse an EVP session that you've recorded. These parts are:

Peak: the highest point above the rest position (the red line through the centre of the wave).

Trough: the lowest point below the rest position.

Amplitude: the maximum displacement of a point of a wave from its rest position.

Wavelength: the distance covered by a full cycle of the wave, usually measured from peak to peak or trough to trough

Another important property of a wave is its frequency, something that is commonly misunderstood in the paranormal field. It can't be measured directly by looking at a waveform, but it can be calculated. The frequency of a waveform is what determines the pitch; we either hear the sound as low pitched or high-pitched. It is measured in hertz (Hz) as the number of complete waves passing a point each second.

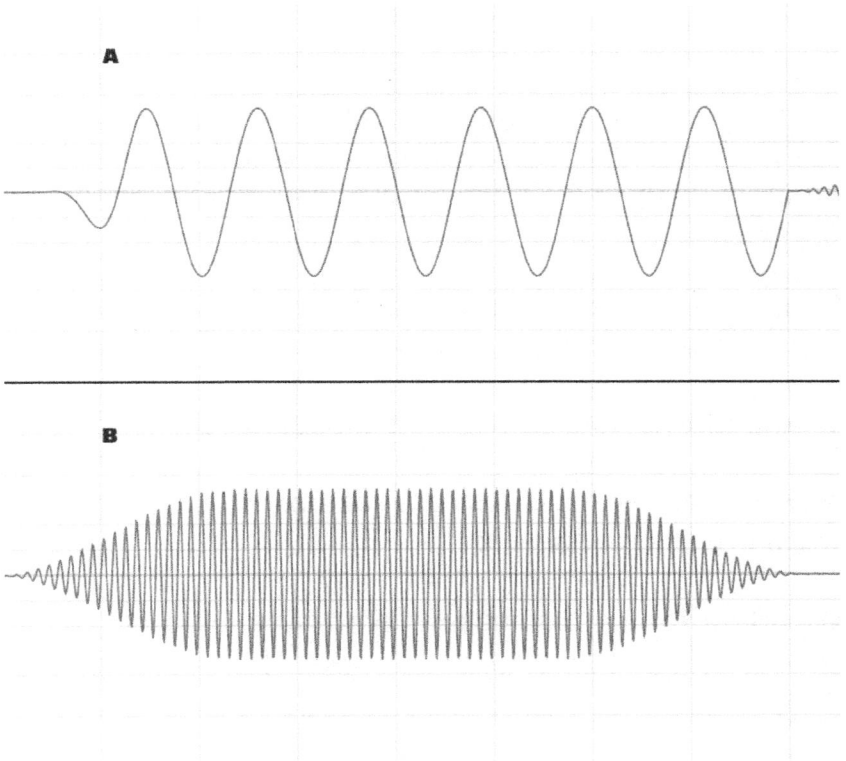

A

B

In the example above, the top waveform (A) has a lower frequency and, therefore, a lower pitch than the bottom waveform (B), which will sound higher pitched.

It is a common misconception that the height of a wave or the presence of peaks is an indication of its frequency. As the diagram above shows, this is not the case, as waves A and B have the same height (amplitude), but the higher number of full cycles of the wave over the same time period in wave B shows that it has a higher frequency than wave A.

Below we can see two sounds, A and B. Both are made up of varying frequencies. Each of the two sounds starts at a low pitch but becomes higher. Wave B is much taller than wave A, which indicates that it has a higher amplitude, measured in decibels (dB).

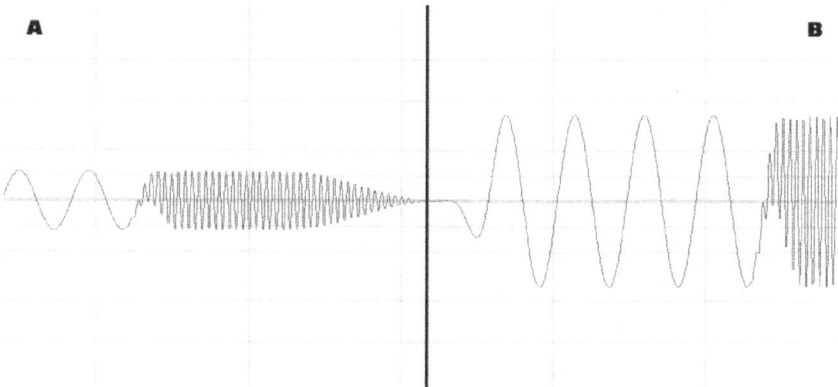

The amplitude of a sound wave determines its volume. We can tell by looking at the diagram above that wave A is quiet while wave B is loud. Therefore, a spike in a recording indicates a loud noise. It's useful to look out for these spikes in audio recorded during an investigation as they may represent an EVP.

When analysing EVPs, you will sometimes need to amplify the recording to see the waveform more clearly and boost the volume of the voice to make it easier to listen back to. Amplifying the audio increases its amplitude, making the wave appear taller, but it doesn't affect the waveform's frequency or wavelength. These two properties are independent of amplitude.

In reality, your waveforms won't be as clear as these examples, especially when dealing with speech, as every voice has a different pitch and words are made up of various different sounds and tones that merge into one erratic waveform that may also include background noise.

Spectral Frequency Display

We know that the height of a waveform tells us the amplitude, or how loud or quiet the sound is. We also know that the horizontal axis of a waveform tells us the duration of the sound, but one thing that cannot be immediately determined from a waveform is the sound's frequency.

However, there is another way to analyse audio that gives you a better understanding of which frequencies are present in a recording, and that's the spectrogram view, sometimes called the spectral frequency display. This is a tool built into Adobe Audition, Audacity, and some other audio software.

In the view, rather than being presented with a waveform, you will see what looks like a heat map, an overview of the audio from which you can determine the volume and different frequencies present in a recording.

Whereas in a waveform view the vertical axis represents the amplitude of the sound, in a spectral frequency display the vertical axis represents the frequency range while the horizontal axis still represents time.

The lighter areas on the display represent louder sounds, and the sound's vertical placement in the graph shows us the frequency of the sound.

If there is a higher density of light patches at the top of the display, then this represents a high-pitched sound. A similarly dense area at the bottom of the display represents a low-pitched sound. This view can make it easier to pick out human voices or low or high-pitched sounds at a glance - something you can't do with a waveform view.

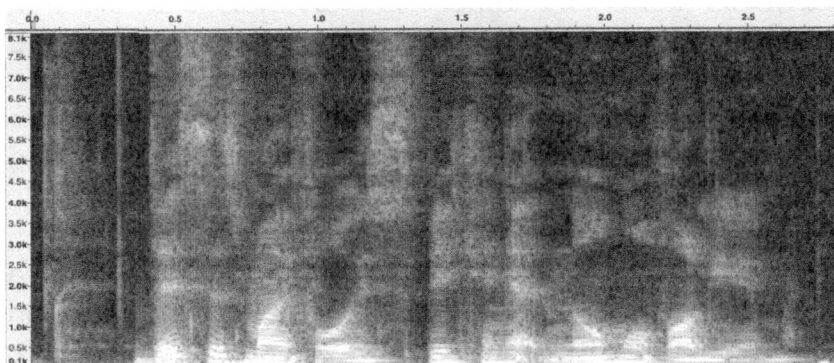

The spectrogram above represents a human voice. Speech has a characteristic look, which you will be able to recognise with a bit of practice, as it always falls within a certain frequency range and therefore has roughly the same vertical placement on a spectrogram.

A male voice has an average frequency of 125 Hz, while a female voice is around 200 Hz. However, we don't speak in a monotone; the pitch of our voices fluctuates, and the voice spans a frequency range up to as high as 8 kHz.

In the example above, you can see that the speech is mostly concentrated below the 500 Hz mark, but there are elements of the speech that reach as high as 6 kHz.

Recognising these patterns will make it easy for you to pick out a voice among the noise. Let's take a look at some noise.

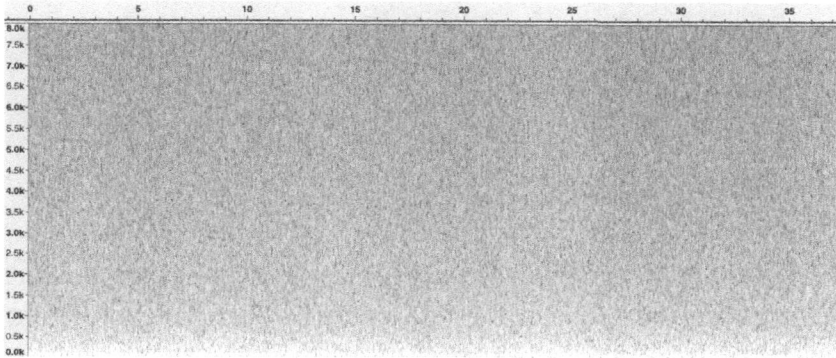

This spectrogram shows pure white noise. It is made up of random sounds across the whole spectrum of frequencies, which gives the spectral frequency display a very uniform look across both the frequency and time axes.

If we mix the previous two examples together so that the voice is playing over the white noise, we get a spectrogram that looks like the example below.

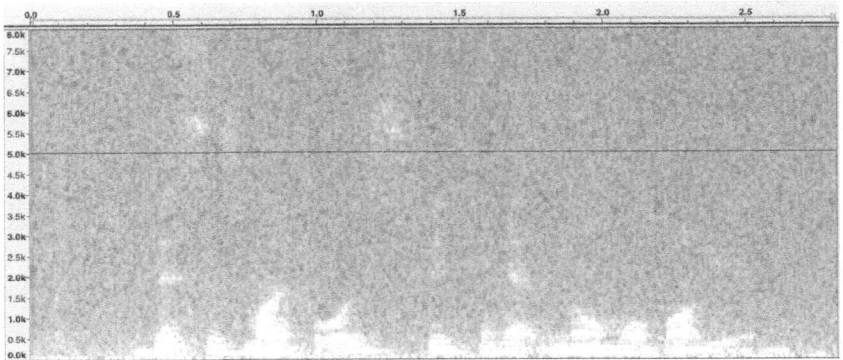

Although there is the same amount of white noise in the example above, it is still clear to see where the voice lies in the recording. Understanding the parts of the spectrogram can be very useful for isolating voices and removing background noise.

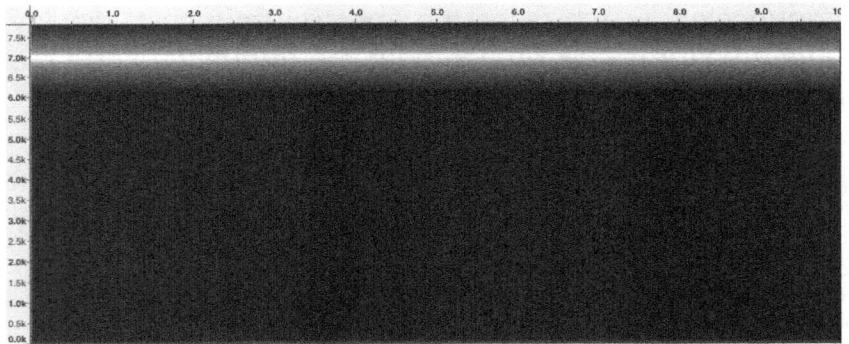

To create the spectrogram above, a pure, high-frequency tone was generated. You can see that the only sound in the recording is the tone, which sits around the 7 kHz mark and lasts for the full duration of the recording. The black portions of the display show that there are no sounds at all within these other frequency ranges.

The spectrogram below was created in the same way but with a 400 Hz tone, which you can see towards the bottom of the spectral display. Again, the large black portions show there are no high-frequency sounds present.

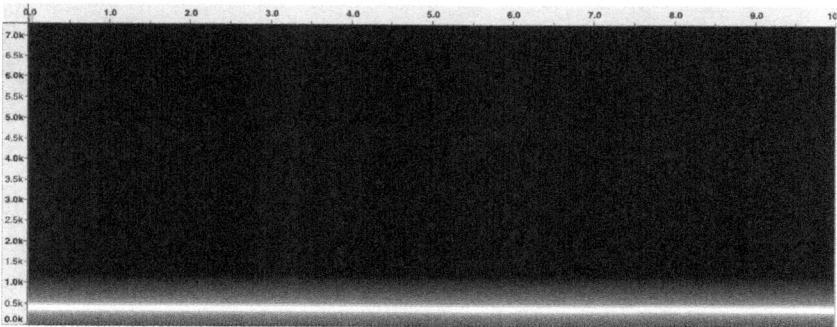

Often, unwanted noise in recordings will be high-pitched hisses or low-end rumbles, so understanding how to identify noises across the frequency ranges will enable you to isolate those sounds and remove them from the recording without affecting the speech you're trying to preserve.

You can remove or reduce these unwanted sounds by highlighting the specific frequency range in the recording and either removing it by pressing delete or cut, or by reducing the volume to zero. Tools like the spot healing brush can also help you to seamlessly remove unwanted sounds with as little disruption to the rest of the recording as possible.

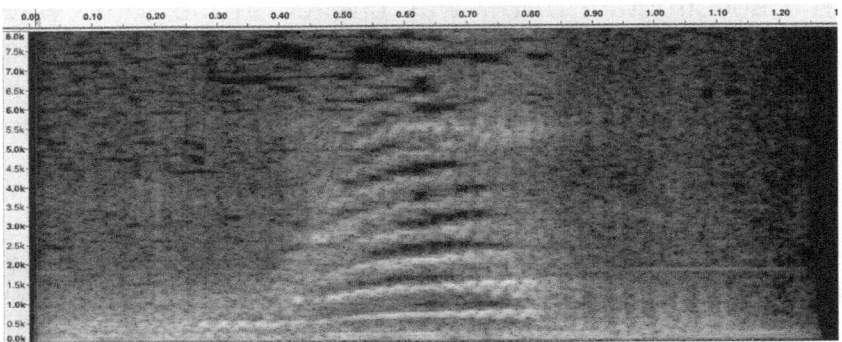

The spectrogram above doesn't show a human voice; it actually represents a cat's meow. You can see that the shapes of the sounds are quite different; they are more uniform in the case of the meow, and the sound is made up of more high-frequency sounds.

Understanding the frequency that sounds are made up of can be very helpful when analysing EVPs. If you capture a voice in your recording, a spectrogram will tell you one of two things: either the voice falls within the normal frequency range of human speech or the voice does not match the tone of a normal human voice.

Since so little is known about the nature of EVPs, where the voices come from, and how they are captured, this information can be interpreted in several different ways.

If a suspected EVP has the signature of a normal human voice, then this could tell you that you have captured the voice of a spirit as they may have sounded in life. It could also tell you that the EVP is the result of radio interference, a real human's voice bleeding through the recording, or the voice of someone present at the investigation.

It may be that the voice is made up of background noise or ambient sounds that have been transformed by having their pitch changed to form words.

If you hear a voice in your recording and then upon inspection in a spectral view determine that it is higher or lower pitched than a normal human voice, then this tells you that it is not the voice of a living person on the investigation.

This leaves you with a few possibilities. The first is that it isn't a voice at all and that this is an example of auditory pareidolia. The second possibility is that spirits don't communicate using the voice they had when they were alive or that, through some strange quirk of recording, the voice's pitch has been shifted.

The other possibility is that sounds from non-human voice ranges have been manipulated to form words. This could have been done in a way that the original pitch of the sound has been preserved but the sounds have been altered to form words or sentences.

Although there's no clear way to tell exactly what is going on in these situations, as a good researcher, you should be aware of the frequency ranges of EVPs, not only to help you debunk or validate evidence but also to look for trends in the evidence captured in order to help further the field of EVP research.

Depending on which software you use, sometimes the spectral view will be a 3D representation of the sound, with frequency, amplitude, and time along the three axes. More commonly, it is a two-dimensional representation as described above, with time along the horizontal axis and frequency on the vertical.

Capturing EVPs Outside the Audible Range

There's often talk in the field of EVP research about capturing voices that are outside the human hearing range, but this is not something that is easily done. It requires specialised equipment and is impractical as part of a paranormal investigation.

The human hearing range, or audible range, is the frequency range that the human ear can detect. The cochlea in the ear is only stimulated by a limited range of frequencies. This means that we can only hear certain frequencies. The range of normal human hearing is 20 Hz–20,000 Hz.

If a voice were outside of this range, it would be speaking at a pitch so low that we can't imagine how that would even sound. On the other hand, if a voice is at a frequency higher than the human audible range, then it would be beyond any piercing high-pitch sound we've ever heard.

There are many cases where an EVP has been captured, and the person playing it back and reviewing the audio has recognised the voice as someone they know. One factor that makes our individual voices recognisable is the frequency we speak at, it determines how low or high pitched our voice is.

When a voice is recorded using an audio capture device and played back, the tone and pitch of the voice remain unchanged in the recording. This tells us that a recording device perfectly preserves the frequency of any voice it records. Therefore, if any recording device were able to capture a voice outside of the audible range, when it was played back, it would be unchanged and would still be beyond the frequency range of the ear - it would remain inaudible.

This means that if an EVP is heard in a recording, it isn't and never has been outside of the human hearing range. If the sound wasn't heard at the time the audio was being recorded but appeared in the recording via some supernatural means, then this is exactly what an EVP is: a mysterious voice captured on a recording that was not heard at the time. The exact mechanism of how the sound is recorded is not understood, but since the recording device would not alter the pitch in anyway, we know that it couldn't have been outside of the human hearing range; it was just unheard at the time.

This doesn't mean that the idea of capturing sounds we can't hear is a ridiculous one; it just means it's not an easy thing to do. Microphones, like the ones you'd find in a smartphone, camera, or digital audio recorder, are designed to capture what the human ear can hear; anything beyond this is just unnecessary data that won't be audible to us in the playback of the recording. Some dictaphones, the type often used on ghost hunts, are even optimised just to capture sounds within the audio range of a human voice; this helps them eliminate extraneous sounds and background noise.

Even if a microphone did have a wider frequency range, the recording device would ignore any sounds outside of the human audible range because it too doesn't want unnecessary data, especially in the case of digital audio where keeping file sizes low is important.

One of the most popular recording formats, and the one used in digital audio recorders that are commonly used to capture EVPs, is the WAV file. It's called a "lossless format," which means that the audio that is stored is an accurate representation of the original sound with no loss of audio quality.

An audio recorder captures packets of audio, usually at 44,100 bits per second; this amount of detail gives it the capacity to capture the entire audible frequency range of 20 Hz to 20 kHz. It will not waste resources capturing any sounds beyond this, as they would be inaudible anyway and would only make the file size bigger unnecessarily.

This means that if you are using a digital audio recorder to try to capture EVPs, you know that the device isn't going to pick up any sounds that you can't hear with your own ears. So, if there is an EVP in your audio recording, then you know it must have been created in one of three ways:

1. The sound was audible at the time of recording and was extremely quiet. It must have been either very close

to the microphone or nearer to the microphone than you were, so it picked up the sound but you didn't. Or the device is more sensitive to low-level noise than your ear.

2. The sound was not audible at the time but has made its way into the recording via a form of electrical interference, which affects either the device's circuitry or storage medium.

3. The sound was somehow imprinted onto the recording via some kind of currently not-understood supernatural method.

The first two possibilities in the list above suggest that the sound might not be an EVP, as in point 3, but this is not strictly the case. In point 1, it could be a spirit making the very quiet sound that the audio recorder picks up, and in point 2, a spirit could be causing the electrical interference.

The very high and very low frequency audio spectrums are an interesting and as yet untapped area of research when it comes to EVPs, perhaps because they come with a high cost of entry due to the need for specialist equipment. Plus, logic dictates that the audible range is where we should focus our attention on capturing EVPs, as this is the frequency range we communicate within in life, so it shouldn't be any different if we can communicate in death.

The equipment needed to investigate the possibility of EVPs outside of our hearing range is different depending on whether you want to capture low-frequency sounds or high-frequency sounds.

Ultra-High Frequency Sound Recording

A very high-frequency sound is called ultrasound; it has a frequency higher than 20,000 Hz, which is outside the upper limit for human hearing.

Ultrasound has several applications in healthcare. It is used to treat kidney stones. The vibrations caused by the ultrasound shake apart kidney stones, breaking them up. It is also used to scan the inside of the body, creating a picture of something that cannot be seen directly, such as an unborn baby in the womb. Ultrasounds are the sounds that bats use to echolocate.

Ultrasound occurs in almost every situation. There is noise around us all the time, but we may not be hearing all of it. Any sort of movement can create a vibration, which in turn creates sound waves; these can be in the ultrasonic range as well as being audible. A lot of the electrical equipment we use on a daily basis emits ultrasound.

Microphones, including those in smartphones and digital audio recorders, are designed specifically to pick up the frequency range that roughly matches the range that the human ear can hear, but most microphones aren't quite as sensitive and fall within this range at about 50 Hz to 18 kHz. Some very expensive specialist microphones are able to pick up audio outside of this range, but you wouldn't find this sort of microphone in any consumer device.

This means that if you want to capture ultrasound, you will need some specialist equipment rather than standard, off-the-shelf recording devices.

There is one tool that might allow you to hear high-frequency sounds without spending a lot of money, and that's a bat detector. These gadgets can be tuned to pick up frequencies from 15,000 Hz to 130,000 Hz, which is far beyond what our ears can hear. These types of detectors are mainly used to pick up ultrasound signals emitted by bats, insects, or other animals.

These devices are capable of translating high frequencies into audible sounds we can hear in real-time. They convert the ultrasound into lower frequencies, which are in the range of human hearing. A headphone output on the device can be used for monitoring the converted sounds in real-time, and some models can also record the sounds onto a memory card.

A bat detector could be used during paranormal investigations to obtain a baseline reading of ultrasound at the location, but also as a means of capturing EVPs at a higher frequency than we can normally hear or capture using a recording device, should they exist in the first place.

Ultra-Low Frequency Sound Recording

Very low-frequency sounds are called infrasound; they have a frequency ranging from 0.1 to 20 Hz. These sounds are below the human range of hearing. While infrasound isn't commonly linked to EVPs, how these sounds affect us is a common area of research for parapsychologists because these low frequency vibrations have been known to cause people to report discomfort in the form of disorientation, feeling panicked, and an increased heart rate and blood pressure. In extreme cases, infrasound has been attributed to feelings of depression, a general feeling of unease, as well as visions of apparitions.

Scientists researching the low frequency noise created by wind turbines and traffic noise discovered the effects of infrasound on humans. They found a link between infrasound and the sensations often described as getting chills down the spine.

As specialist audio equipment is required to detect infrasound, it can be hard to eliminate this from your investigation. However, keeping doors and windows closed will help to keep these frequencies out of the building. It should also be noted that some machinery and even fans can produce the low frequencies associated with infrasound. For this reason, care should be taken to turn off any electrical equipment that could interfere with your investigation.

The link between infrasound and paranormal activity was first researched by some of the early paranormal investigators, including Harry Price, who would make a basic tilt switch using mercury (similar to a modern accelerometer in a phone) in order to detect tremors that could produce infrasound waves. It was the subject of Vic Tandy's 1980 discover relating to a standing wave in his lab being responsible for perceived paranormal activity.

Infrasound is very hard to record; it's not just a case of buying an expensive microphone, as even the best microphone is designed to only capture audible sounds. Although there are purpose-built infrasound mics available, like those manufactured by Bruel & Kjaer, they will set you back around $500. You'll also need a preamp and specialised recording equipment. There's also specialist infrasound monitoring equipment, like the Earthworks QTC-1, which will set you back around $1,000.

It might be possible to construct your own infrasound monitor in a similar way to Harry Price by using a large membrane or diaphragm with a diameter of at least 60 cm or by using a long hollow pipe that could be compressed when the sound hits it. You'd then need to attach a sensitive accelerometer to measure the vibration of either apparatus. Although this approach might work, it wouldn't give you a recording as such, but you'd be able to monitor the amplitude of the infrasound waves using an oscilloscope.

EVP Classification

Unlike a lot of evidence of the paranormal, it's common practise to grade voices captured as EVPs. There is one commonly agreed upon classification scale with defined requirements to help investigators determine which category of EVP they've captured.

According to the Association TransCommunication (ATransC), any form of ITC, including EVP, can be split into two types:

Type 1: Transformative - manipulation of dissimilar sounds

Type 2: Opportunistic - selective use of existing voices

These two types of EVP actually have more to do with the environment the EVP was captured in than the voice recording itself.

Type 1 EVPs are transient sounds of a pitch matching a human voice that spontaneously appear amongst background noise or sounds of a differing pitch. This could be the sound of a voice coming through amongst the hiss or hum that is the ambient sound of the room, or a voice with a similar tone to a human voice heard amongst white noise.

In Type 1 EVPs, the voice is made up of background noise that has been transformed. Random and chaotic background noise is manipulated; its pitch is changed, and words are formed from the ambient sounds. This would cover most EVPs captured during a paranormal investigation, including those captured on audio recorders, whether additional noise was generated or not.

Type 2 EVPs appear within persistent or constant sounds that are already human voices. The EVP is made up opportunistically by using existing words or word parts to form new words or sentences.

For an EVP to be classified as Type 2, it must have been captured using a device that has voices being inputted into it. This could either be via the device's microphone or another audio input, or via a radio modulator (AM or FM) in the case of a spirit box.

The input sound that is being used to form the EVP could include a conversation taking place in the room or someone talking on the radio. It could also be pre-recorded voices that are being played in. It's a fairly common technique for EVP researchers to use audio tracks featuring chanting, foreign languages, or abstract voices during EVP sessions. The same method is also employed by electronic speech synthesis systems like the Ovilus and Echovox, which spew out the random phonics that make up words.

Each of these two types of EVP is divided into subclasses, and it is these that are most commonly referred to by paranormal investigators. You may have heard someone say that a capture is a "Class A EVP," for example. There are a few different scales used to classify EVPs.

All of these scales categorise EVPs as A, B, or C. With class A being the best quality or less objective. Class A EVPs are much stronger evidence than classes B or C. Class C EVPs are generally not easily heard or understood; therefore, it's difficult to determine whether the voice is of paranormal origin or not.

Generally, class A EVPs are clear to hear without explanation, while class B EVPs may require directions. Class C EVPs are vague and mostly obscured by noise.

The Raudive Scale

Konstantin Raudive was the first prominent EVP researcher to attempt to categorise the voices he captured into three classes of audibility. He described the scale he used in his 1968 book, 'Breakthrough: An Amazing Experiment in Electronic Communication with the Dead,' which was printed in English in 1971.

He wrote, "This grading and my comments are but a rough guide in the present stage of our approach to the psycho-acoustic aspect of the investigation."

Raudive's scale was not widely adopted but is a forerunner to more popular EVP classification methods. Raudive ranked EVPs based on the ease of hearing the voice; later classification systems would take into account the context of the words spoken by the voice.

The Raudive Scale	
Class A	Voices can be heard and identified by anyone with normal hearing and knowledge of the language spoken; no special training of the ear is needed to detect them.
Class B	Voices speak more rapidly and more softly, but are still quite plainly audible to a trained and attentive ear.
Class C	Voices give us a great deal of information and much paranormal data.

Unfortunately, these can be heard only in fragments, even by a trained ear, but with improved technical aids, it may eventually become possible to hear and demonstrate these voices, which lie beyond our range of hearing, without trouble.

Raudive wrote that most of his recordings fell into Class A; he noted that "it is easy to make tape copies of 'A' voices, and they can be repeated as often as desired. Thus, I have analyzed roughly 25,000 voices according to speech content, language and rhythm. By this method of repetition, the acoustic reality of the voices can be established beyond doubt, and hallucinations of the ear are excluded."

As Raudive points out, Class B voices can be harder to identify and he suggests that practising analysing EVPs might help; "the ability to differentiate increases with practice, but this is a slow and wearisome process. For this reason it is difficult to use non-regular participants for experimental purposes with class 'B' voices."

The Estep System

The Raudive Scale was soon replaced by a classification system that was clearer and took into account filtering and amplification where needed. The first iteration of this system was first popularised in Sarah Estep's 1988 book, 'Voices of Eternity'. The scale became a global standard for EVP classification.

The Estep System	
Class A	Voices are loud and clear, they can be duplicated onto other tapes. Can be heard without headphones.
Class B	Voices aren't as loud and clear, and can often be heard without headphones.
Class C	Voices are faint or whispery. Headphones must be worn to hear them, and rarely can all the words be interpreted.

Contrary to Raudive's scale, the majority of the voices that Estep captured fell into the Class C category. However, like Raudive's scale, Estep's system soon became outdated and was updated by the AA-EVP. The Association's system of classification was based on the quality and clarity of the EVP, and it also aimed to remove subjectivity, something previous classification scales hadn't attempted to tackle.

The AA-EVP System	
Class A	EVP is a message that can be heard without headphones and that people can generally agree on its content.

The AA-EVP System	
Class B	EVP requires headphones to distinguish message content and not everyone will agree on the message.
Class C	EVP requires headphones, often needs amplification and filtering and will seldom even be heard by others.

The KM System

Although the AA-EVP's classification are commonly used still, today the most widely used and accepted classification system is the KM EVP system. It is named after EVP researchers, Doug Kelley and Jari Mikkola.

Kelley and Mikkola's system is more useful when it comes to rating not only the quality of the EVP recording, but also the message contained within it, as this is where any evidence to support paranormal contact will lie. Their scale takes things a step further than the previous classification methods by taking into account the context of the message, how meaningful it is, and how easy it is to comprehend.

The KM System

Class 1 *Interactive*	Spirit voice is a direct response to a human statement, question, action, activity, or spirit voices respond to each other: • Most or all of the words are clear and intelligible, with or without headphones • Spirit voice communicates comprehensible and existentially meaningful expressions of thoughts, feelings, emotions, opinions, actions, or intentions
Class 2 *Non Interactive*	Voice is a general statement and not a direct response to a statement, question, action, or activity, by humans: • Most or all of the words are generally clear and understandable, with or without headphones • Spirit voice communication is comprehensible and existentially a meaningful expression of thoughts, feelings, emotions, opinions, actions, or intentions

The KM System	
Class 3 *Non Speech*	Spirit voice is a sound other than the spoken word: • Growls, screams, humming, etc • Musical instruments, TV, radio, concerts, footsteps, rapping, banging, barking, etc
Class 4 *Null*	The EVP contains nothing of value in understanding the spirit realm or spirit psychology: • Words are unintelligible, with or without headphones • Spirit voice does not communicate comprehensible and existentially meaningful expressions of thoughts, feelings, emotions, opinions, actions, or intentions, although the word(s) may be intelligible

Afterword

As you close the final pages of 'Whispers From The Other Side,' I hope that you feel inspired to continue exploring the mysteries of the paranormal world. You now have the tools to delve deeper into the realm of electronic voice phenomena and paranormal communication.

Remember that the journey towards discovering the truth about the paranormal is ongoing and ever-evolving. There is no one-size-fits-all approach, and what works for one person may not work for another. The most important thing is to remain open-minded, stay grounded, and maintain a healthy dose of skepticism.

I also want to thank you for choosing to read my book. I have been passionate about the paranormal for many years, and it brings me great joy to share my knowledge and experiences with others. I hope that my writing has sparked your curiosity and provided you with valuable insights into the world of EVPs.

If you're interested in exploring more paranormal topics, please visit Higgypop.com, where you'll find a wealth of resources and information on ghost hunting, demonology, and other paranormal phenomena. I also invite you to check out my other books in this series, which delve deeper into specific aspects of the paranormal world.

Thank you again for reading 'Whispers From The Other Side.' May your journey towards uncovering the truth be filled with wonder, discovery, and above all, an unwavering commitment to the pursuit of knowledge.

Made in the USA
Las Vegas, NV
16 May 2025